THE COLOGNE MANI CODEX
(P. Colon. inv. nr. 4780)
"Concerning the Origin of his Body"

translated by
Ron Cameron and
Arthur J. Dewey

Scholars Press

Distributed by
Scholars Press
PO Box 5207
Missoula, Montana 59806

THE COLOGNE MANI CODEX
(P. Colon. inv. nr. 4780)
"Concerning the Origin of his Body"
translated by
Ron Cameron
and
Arthur J. Dewey

Library of Congress Cataloging in Publication Data

Cologne Mani codex. English & Greek.
    The Cologne Mani codex (P. Colon. inv. nr.
4780).

    (Early Christian literature series ; 3 ISSN 0145-
322X) (Texts and translations ; 15 ISSN 0145-3203)
    The original 5th cent. A.D. miniature parchment
is in the Papyrussammlung des Instituts fur
Altertumskunde in Cologne and has running title:
Peri tes gennes tou somatos autou.
    Bibliography: p.
    1. Mani, 3d cent. 2. Manichaeism—Biography. 3.
Manichaeism. I. Mani, 3d cent. II. Cameron, Ron. III.
Dewey, Arthur J. IV. Title. V. Series. VI. Series:
Society of Biblical Literature. Texts and translations ;
15.
BT1410.M28C6413   299   79-14743
ISBN 0-89130-311-1
ISBN 0-89130-312-X pbk.

Printed in The United States of America
1   2   3   4   5
Printing Department
University of Montana
Missoula, Montana 59812

THE COLOGNE MANI CODEX

Society of Biblical Literature

TEXTS AND TRANSLATIONS
EARLY CHRISTIAN LITERATURE SERIES

edited by
Birger A. Pearson

Texts and Translations Number 15
Early Christian Literature Series 3

THE COLOGNE MANI CODEX
(P. Colon, inv. nr. 4780)
"Concerning the Origin of his Body"
translated by
Ron Cameron
and
Arthur J. Dewey

PREFACE TO THE SERIES

TEXTS AND TRANSLATIONS is a project of the Committee on Research and Publications of the Society of Biblical Literature. The purpose of this project is to make available in convenient and inexpensive format ancient texts which are not easily accessible but are of importance to scholars and students of "biblical literature" as broadly defined by the Society. Reliable modern English translations accompany the texts. It is not a primary aim of these publications to provide authoritative new critical editions, nor to furnish extensive commentaries. The editions are regarded as provisional, and individual volumes may be replaced in the future as better textual evidence becomes available.

The following subseries have been established thus far:

PSEUDEPIGRAPHA, edited by Robert A. Kraft
(University of Pennsylvania)

GRECO-ROMAN RELIGION, edited by Hans Dieter Betz
(University of Chicago)

EARLY CHRISTIAN LITERATURE, edited by Birger A.
Pearson (University of California, Santa
Barbara)

The EARLY CHRISTIAN LITERATURE SERIES is intended to include texts from Christian literature through the early patristic period, with the exception of those that

belong properly in the PSEUDEPIGRAPHA SERIES. This and
earlier volumes in the series have been selected, prepared, and edited in consultation with an editorial
committee consisting of Stephen Benko (California State
University at Fresno), John Gager (Princeton University),
William R. Schoedel (University of Illinois at Urbana),
and Wilhelm Wuellner (Pacific School of Religion).

Birger A. Pearson, Editor

TABLE OF CONTENTS

INTRODUCTION

The Cologne Mani Codex (*CMC*) is a miniature parchment of the fifth century C.E. which provides new information on Mani's life in a baptist sect in southern Babylonia. In 1969, through the expert work of A. Fackelmann, the Codex was successfully opened and rendered readable. A. Henrichs and L. Koenen published in 1970 a preliminary overview of the Codex, along with a discussion of the salient issues arising from it, in the *Zeitschrift für Papyrologie und Epigraphik*. Since then, in the same journal, a critical edition, German translation, and critical notes of the first ninety-nine pages have been furnished by them in two installments (1975; 1978). The remaining material awaits future publication. It was at the suggestion of A. Henrichs that we took up the task of a first English translation.

On paleographical grounds the Codex can be assigned to the late fourth or early fifth century. Even in size the Codex is remarkable, for it appears to be the smallest book ever found. This parchment codex or "pocketbook" numbers 192 pages in length, featuring eight quires of 24 pages each. The parchment, when closed, measures 4.5 cm x 3.5 cm; the writing measures 3.5 cm x 2.5 cm. Each page has regularly 23 lines. The first twenty-four pages are fragmentary, with pages 116 to the end in even poorer condition.

1

The **language** of the Codex appears at first to be relatively simple. Yet translation difficulties arise for two reasons. First, the Greek text is translated from a Syriac original. Second, the particular baptist and Manichaean terms have theological nuances which require attention.

The latter point can be seen even in the title of the Codex. Running along the top of the pages of the Codex (except for its omission on pp. 94-95) we find the words περὶ τῆς γέννης τοῦ σώματος αὐτοῦ ("Concerning the Origin of his Body"). These words appear quite straight-forward and would seem to refer to the life of Mani taken up in the Codex. However, the title may well have broader theological significance. For one soon realizes that these biographical accounts of Mani are redacted not along genuinely biographical lines but according to theo-logical, or more specifically, ecclesiological principles. Thus, the title of the Codex may well refer to the origin of the Manichaean Church. An interesting and pertinent parallel is the Pauline formulation of the Church as the Body of Christ.

The Codex seems to have undergone three stages of redaction in coming to its present state (cf. Henrichs, "Literary Criticism ..." below). The original layer may well yield Mani's own autobiographical quotations. These were taken up into a second stage under the names of Mani's disciples. In turn these sources were compiled by an unknown author, who, despite his anonymity, imposed a

particular format upon the material. By noting certain
editorial transitions and breaks, along with the narrated
progress of Mani's spiritual initiation, the Codex can be
seen as divided into five thematic units, giving an
account of the first twenty-four years of the life of
Mani.

These units appear to be arranged in a concentric,
"onionskin," fashion. Thus, the two outside layers,
Parts I and V, parallel each other, while II and IV do
likewise. Part III rests in the center of this arrange-
ment. The first section (pp. 2-14), telling of Mani from
years four to twelve, comes from three different sources
and provides two full-fledged conversion accounts. The
fifth section (pp. 116-92), meanwhile, contains a long
but extremely fragmentary itinerary of Mani's first
missionary journey. Most emphatically gnostic is the
second section (pp. 14-72), featuring such narrative
forms as epiphanies, catalogues of existential questions,
rhetorical declarations of identity, and revelation dis-
courses and dialogues. Accounts of Mani's separation
from the baptists, his call to be a missionary, and
instructions for the foundation of Manichaeism as a
world religion, all in dialogue form, comprise the fourth
section (pp. 99-116). Finally, the midsection (pp. 72-
99), composed of five separate excerpts, features the
dramatic break with the baptists. Here, in this most
important part, we are given valuable information of this
transition, wherein the latent differences between Mani

4

and the baptists erupted into theological debate.

The importance of the Cologne Mani Codex cannot be overestimated for the history of religions. For the Codex provides the only Greek primary source for Manichaeism. Now we have not only new reports and accounts of the early life of Mani, but even additional evidence for a Gospel of Mani. Indeed, many of the excerpts resemble a proto-gospel in a raw state, along with apocalypses and aretalogical material. Moreover, the origin of Manichaeism becomes quite complex, since we now possess convincing evidence of the connection of Mani's baptists with Elchasai, the alleged founder of a predominantly Jewish-Christian sect. And, most of all, we are privy to new and unparalleled information on the organization, ritual practices, and theology of the baptist sect in which Mani was reared.

In light of this importance and in order to make this document more widely available, we have decided to print the first three sections. The final two parts, along with an *Index Verborum*, will appear after the completion of the critical edition by Henrichs and Koenen. It is quite appropriate to extend our deepest gratitude to A. Henrichs for continued support, criticism, and encouragement. For the patient and meticulous assistance of J. Strugnell and the helpful suggestions of B. Pearson we are grateful. To G. MacRae, who encouraged us and helped in the editorial process, we express our thanks.

We also wish to thank G. Bisbee and J. Burnich for their careful and precise typing of a difficult manuscript. Lastly, these translation "twins" acknowledge their female σύζυγοι by dedicating this work to the ones who sustained the project with their sympathy and the necessary afternoon cocoa.

SELECT BIBLIOGRAPHY

Henrichs, A. "Mani and the Babylonian Baptists: a historical confrontation," *Harvard Studies in Classical Philology* (=*HSCP*) 77 (1973) 23-59.

————. "The Cologne Mani Codex Reconsidered," *HSCP* 83 (1979, at press).

————. "Literary Criticism of the Cologne Mani Codex," *Proceedings of the International Conference on Gnosticism at Yale.* Leiden: Brill (at press).

————. "'Thou Shalt not Kill a Tree': Greek, Manichaean and Indian Tales," *Bulletin of the American Society of Papyrologists* 16 (1979) 85-108.

Henrichs, A., and Koenen, L. "Ein griechischer Mani-Codex (P. Colon. inv. nr. 4780)," *Zeitschrift für Papyrologie und Epigraphik* (=*ZPE*) 5 (1970) 97-217.

————. "Der Kölner Mani-Kodex (P. Colon. inv. nr. 4780). ΠΕΡΙ ΤΗΣ ΓΕΝΝΗΣ ΤΟΥ ΣΩΜΑΤΟΣ ΑΥΤΟΥ. Edition der Seiten 1-72," *ZPE* 19 (1975) 1-85.

————. "Der Kölner Mani-Kodex (P. Colon. inv. nr. 4780). ΠΕΡΙ ΤΗΣ ΓΕΝΝΗΣ ΤΟΥ ΣΩΜΑΤΟΣ ΑΥΤΟΥ. Edition der Seiten 72,8-99,9," *ZPE* 32 (1978) 87-199.

Koenen, L. "Das Datum der Offenbarung und Geburt Manis," *ZPE* 8 (1971) 247-50.

————. "Augustine and Manichaeism in Light of the Cologne Mani Codex," *Illinois Classical Studies* 3 (1978) 154-95.

————. "From Baptism to the Gnosis of Manichaeism," *Proceedings of the International Conference on Gnosticism at Yale.* Leiden: Brill (at press).

Rudolph, K. "Die Bedeutung des Kölner Mani-Codex für die Manichäismusforschung: vorläufige Anmerkungen," *Mélanges d'histoire des religions offerts à Henri-Charles Puech* (Paris: Presses Universitaires de France, 1974) 471-86.

SIGLA

[ ]   Square brackets indicate a lacuna in the manuscript. When the text cannot be reconstructed,
three dots are placed within the brackets,
regardless of the length of the lacuna. Words or
phrases placed within the brackets indicate the
suggested reconstructions of the editors.

< >   Pointed brackets indicate a correction by the
editors of a scribal omission or error.

( )   Parentheses indicate material supplied by the
translators. Numbers placed within parentheses
indicate the respective page and line numbers of
the Greek text. Words or phrases placed within
parentheses indicate translational clarifications
of the ambiguities of the Greek text.

. . .   Three dots placed at the beginning or end of
translated sections indicate a lacuna which
cannot be reconstructed, regardless of its
length. Greek letters with single dots under
them indicate those letters in the Codex which
are mutilated and concerning which there is some
doubt as to their readings.

{ }   Braces indicate Greek letters which the editors
consider erroneous or superfluous.

(2.2)[1] ". . . [κατ]ὰ βραχὺ β[ρα]χὺ | . . . .[. .]ον· ασεβ[. . . .] |
(4) σοι ἔδειξ[α . . . .] | ἀπὸ πολλ[ῶν . . . . . ἔ]ϛτα[ι] |
δέ σοι μεγα[λοπ]ρεπῶς | καὶ ὀφθαλμοφανέστα| (8)τα θεωρῆσαι
τὸ μυστήρι|ον ἐκεῖνο." καὶ τότε ὁ | ἄγγελος ἀπεκρύβη ἀ|[πὸ]

. . .

(3.2) . . . [διὰ σθ]ένους [τῶν] ἁγ|[γέ]λων ἐφυλάχθην καὶ |
(4) τῶν δυνάμεων τῆς ὁ|σιότητος τῶν ἐγχειρι|σθεισῶν τὴν
ἐμὴν πα|ραφυλακήν, οἵ καὶ ἀνέ|(8)θρεψαν με δι᾽ ὀπτασιῶν |
καὶ σημείων ὧν ὑπεδεί|κνυόν μοι μικρῶν καὶ | βραχυτάτων
καθὼς ἐ|(12)δυνάμην ὑποφέρειν. |

Ποτὲ μὲν γὰρ ἀϛτραπῆς | δίκην ἐφίϰεϛ[ο] . . .

(4.3) . . . ἠσφαλίζετο δέ | με καὶ περὶ ταύτης τῆς |
δυνάμεως τῆς ἐν θλίψει | ἐστώσης.

Πλεῖσται δέ εἰσιν ὀπτασί|(8)αι καὶ τὰ θεάματα
μέγι|στα ἃ ὑπέδειξέν μοι κα|τ᾽ ἐκεῖνον πάντα τὸν | καιρὸν
τῆς νεότητός | (12) μου. ἐγὼ δὲ ἐν σιωπῆι | .[. . . .
ἔμει]να. ἐὰν μή | . . .

CONCERNING THE ORIGIN OF HIS BODY

(2.2)[1] ". . . little by little [. . . I] (4) have shown you [unholy . . .] from many [. . .]. But you will be able to behold (8) that mystery magnificently and most lucidly." And then the angel was hidden [from] . . .

(3.2) . . . I (Mani) was protected [through] the might of [the] angels and (4) the powers of holiness who were entrusted with my safekeeping, and (8) they nourished me with visions and signs which they made known to me, slight and quite brief, as far as (12) I was able to bear.

For sometimes like a flash of lightning he [came] . . .

(4.3) . . . but he was reassuring (4) me also about this power which is steadfast in affliction.

Now very many are the visions (8) and exceedingly great are the sights which he showed to me during all that time of my youth. (12) But I [. . . remained] in silence. Except . . .

---

[1]Page 1 is too fragmentary for translation.

10

(5.3) . . . σὺν σοφίαι καὶ | (4) [εὐ]μηχανίαι περιερ|[χό]-
μενος μεταξὺ αὐ|[τ]ῶν καὶ κατέχων τὴν | ἀνάπαυσιν[2] καὶ μὴ
ἀδι|(8)κῶν μηδὲ ἀγιῶν μη|δὲν μηδὲ ἐξακολου|θῶν τῶι νόμωι
τῶν | βαπτιστῶν μηδὲ πα|(12)ραπλησίως αὐτοῖς δια|λεγόμενος.
Σαλμαῖ[ο]ς ὁ [ἀσκητής]
. . .

(6.2) ". . . αὐτῶι.[3] ἀλλ᾿ οὐδὲ [λάχα]|να λαμβάνεις ἀπὸ τ[οῦ]|
(4) κήπου, ἀλλ᾿ οὐδὲ ξύλα | πρὸς τὴν χρῆσιν αὐτοῦ | φέρεις."
  ᾿Ηνάγκαζεν δέ με ἐκεῖ|(8)νος ὁ βαπτιστὴς λέγων· |
"ἀναστὰς ἐλθὲ σὺν ἐμοὶ | εἰς τὸν τόπον ἔνθα ἔστιν | ξύλα
καὶ δεξάμενος | (12) φέρε." ἀπερχομένων | δὲ ἡμῶν εἴς
τινα φοί|[νικα ἀ]νέβη ἐκεῖνος . . .

(7.2) . . . "ἐὰν τὸν μό|[χθο]ν εἴρξηις ἐξ ἡμῶν, | (4)
[οὐχ] ἅμα τῶι φονεῖ ἀ|[πο]λῆι." πρὸς ἐμὲ τότε ἐ|κεῖνος ὁ
βαπτιστὴς φό|βωι συσχεθεὶς σὺν θο|(8)ρύβωι κατῆλθεν
ἐξ αὐ|τοῦ καὶ πρὸς τοὺς ἐμοὺς | πόδας ἔπεσεν λέγων· |
"οὐκ ἐγίνωσκον ὅτι τοῦ|(12)το τὸ ἀπόρρητον μυ|στήριον
παρὰ σοί ἐστιν. | πόθεν δέ σοι ἀπεκαλύ|φθη ἡ περι[ωδυνία
φοί]|νι[κος];" . . .

(5.3) . . . with wisdom and (4) skill (I was) going about in their midst, keeping the Rest,[2] neither doing wrong, (8) nor inflicting pain, nor following the Law of the Baptists, nor (12) speaking in the way they did.

Salmaios the [Ascetic]

. . .

(6.2) ". . . to [him].[3] But neither do you take [vegetables] from [the] (4) garden, nor do you carry wood for his use."

But that Baptist constrained me, (8) saying: "Get up and come with me to the place where there is wood; take it and (12) carry it." We went away to a certain [date-palm tree], and he climbed up . . .

(7.2) . . . "If you keep the [pain] away from us (trees), (4) you will [not perish] with the murderer." Then that Baptist, gripped by fear of me, (8) came down from it in confusion, and fell at my feet and said: "I did not know that this (12) secret mystery is with you. Whence was the [agony of the date-palm tree] revealed to you?" . . .

---

[2]"Rest": Cf. Henrichs, "Mani and the Babylonian Baptists," 48-50.

[3]Translators read, with the critical text: αὐτῶι.

(8.1) ". . . ὅ[τε δὲ ἡ φοῖνιξ εἶπεν] | πρὸς σὲ τοῦτο, πῶ[ς κατ]|εφοβήθης καὶ τὴν [χροι]|(4)ὰν μετέβαλες; ἐκ[εῖνος] | μεθ᾽ οὗ πάντα τὰ φ[υτ]ὰ | λαλεῖ ποσαπλασίονα | κινηθήσεται;" | (8) ἐξεπέπληκτο τοίνυν | κατεχόμενος ὑπὸ θαύ|ματος δι᾽ ἐμέ. ἔλεγέν | μοι· "φύλαξον τὸ μυστή|(12)ριον τοῦτο, μηδενὶ ἐ|ξείπῃς, ἵνα μή τις φθο|νέσας ἀπολέσει σε." . . .

(9.1) . . . ἀναπαύσ[εως ἔ]νε|[κεν], ἔλεγεν πρὸς ἐμὲ εἷς | [τῶ]ν ἀρχηγῶν τοῦ νό|(4)μου αὐτῶν θεωρήσας | με λάχανα ἀπὸ τοῦ κή|που μὴ λαμβάνοντα | ἀλλ᾽ ἀπαιτοῦντα αὐτοὺς | (8) ἐν λόγωι εὐσεβεί|ας.[4] ἔλεγέν μοι· "σὺ τίνος | χάριν οὐκ ἔλαβες λά|χανα ἀπὸ τοῦ κήπου | (12) ἀλλ᾽ ἐν μέρει εὐσεβείας | αἰτεῖς παρ᾽ ἐμοῦ;" καὶ με|τὰ τὸ εἰπεῖν δὲ ἐκ[εῖ]|νον τὸν βαπ[τιστὴν] | πρὸς [ἐμέ] . . .

(10.1) . . . [κ]αὶ ἐτάκ[η ὁλοφυρό]|μενον παραπλησ[ίως ἀν]|θρωπείοις προσώ[ποις] | (4) καὶ ὡσεὶ παιδίοις. οὐαὶ ο[ὺ]|αὶ δὲ τὸ αἷμα κατεκέχυτο | τοῦ τόπου τοῦ κοπέντος | διὰ τῆς δρεπάνης ἧς με|(8)τὰ χεῖρας εἶχεν. ἔκραζον | δὲ καὶ ἀνθρωπείαι φω|νῆι διὰ τὰς πλήξεις αὐ|τῶν. ὁ δὲ βαπτιστὴς | (12) πάνυ ἐκινήθη ἐφ᾽ οἷς | ἐθεώρησεν

(8.1) (Mani is now speaking) ". . . [When the date-palm tree said] this to you, why did you become [greatly] frightened and (4) change your complexion? How much more will [that one], with whom all the [plants] speak, be disturbed?" (8) Thereupon he was dumbfounded, beside himself in amazement over me. He said to me: "Guard (12) this mystery, tell it to no one, lest someone become envious and destroy you." . . .

(9.1) . . . [for the sake of the] Rest, one of the leaders of their Law spoke to me, (4) having observed that I did not take vegetables from the garden, but instead asked them (for the vegetables) as (8) a pious gift.[4] He said to me: "Why did you not take vegetables from the garden, (12) but instead ask me (for them) as a pious gift?" After that Baptist had spoken to [me] . . .

(10.1) . . . [it] wasted away, [wailing] like human beings, (4) and, as it were, like children. Alas! Alas! The blood was streaming down from the place cut by the pruning hook which (8) he held in his hands. And they were crying out in a human voice on account of their blows. The Baptist (12) was greatly moved by what he saw,

----

[4] "Pious gift": Cf. Henrichs, "Mani and the Babylonian Baptists," 36 n. 48.

14

καὶ ἐλθὼν | [π]ρ[ό]σθεν μου προσέπε|[σεν. ὁπ]ηνίκα τοίνυν
. . .

(11.1) . . . μέ|[χρι] τετάρτου ἔτους· | [τότ]ε εἰσήλασα εἰς
τὸ δό|(4)γμα τῶν βαπτιστῶν | ἐν ὧι καὶ ἀνετράφην | κατὰ
τὸ νέον τοῦ σώμα|τος φυλασσόμενος διὰ | (8) τοῦ σθένους
τῶν φωτει|νῶν ἀγγέλων καὶ δυνά|μεων τῶν ἰσχυροτά|των
αἵτινες ἐντολὴν | (12) ἔσχον πρὸς τοῦ Ἰησοῦ τῆς | εἴλης
παραφυλακῆς χά|ριν. αὐτῶν τότε παραχρῆμ[α] [5] . . .

(12.) . . . [ἐκ] | (1) τῶν ὑδάτων π[ρόσωπον] | ἀνθρώπου
ὤφθη μοι ὑ[ποδει]|κνύον διὰ τῆς χειρ[ὸς] | (4) τὴν
ἀνάπαυσιν ὡς ἂν | μὴ ἁμάρτω καὶ πόνον | ἐπάγω εἰς αὐτόν.
τοῦ|τον τὸν τρόπον ἀπό τε|(8)τάρτου ἔτους καὶ μέ|χρις οὗ
ἔφθασα εἰς τὸ ἀ|κμαῖον τοῦ σώματός | μου ἐν ταῖς χερσὶν
τῶν | (12) ἁγνοτάτων ἀγγέλων | καὶ τῶν τῆς ὁσιότητος |
δυνάμεων περιτηρού|[μενος ἔλα]θον . . .

(13.2) . . . ἄλλοτε δὲ ὡς σύ|ζυγος φωνὴ ἐκ τοῦ ἀέ|(4)ρος
διελέγετο πρὸς ἐ|μὲ λέγουσα· "ῥῶσόν σου | τὴν δύναμιν
καὶ κρά|τυνον τὴν φρένα καὶ | (8) πρόσδεξαι πάντα τὰ
ἀ|ποκαλυπτόμενά σοι." | καὶ πάλιν ἔλεγεν τὸ

and he came and fell down before me. When, then, . . .

(11.1) . . . until the fourth year. Then I (Mani) gained
entrance to the (4) teaching of the Baptists in which I
was reared, while my body was young, being guarded by
(8) the might of the Light-angels and the exceedingly
strong powers, who had a command (12) from Jesus, the
Splendor, for (my) safekeeping. They, then, immediately[5]
. . .

(12.1) . . . [from] the waters [a face] of a man appeared
to me, showing with his hand (4) the Rest, so that I
might not sin and bring trouble to him. In this way,
from my (8) fourth year until I attained my bodily
maturity, by the hands of the (12) most pure angels and
the powers of holiness I was protected [without anyone's
notice] . . .

(13.2) . . . at another time a voice, like that of the
Twin, (4) spoke to me out of the air, saying: "Strengthen
your power, make your mind firm, and (8) receive all that
is about to be revealed to you." And again, he said the

---

[5]After χάριν, translators read, with the critical
text: αὐτῶν τότε παραχρῆμ[α.

αὐ|τό· "ῥῶσον τὴν δύναμιν | (12) καὶ στῆσόν σου τὴν φρέ|να
καὶ ὑπόστα πάντα | τὰ ἐρχόμενα ἐπὶ σέ." . . .

(14.1) ". . . ὑπὸ μεγάλων [πατέρων] | προεβλήθημεν." |
        Βαρ<α>ίης ὁ διδάσκαλος. |

    (4) Ἔλεγεν ὁ κύριός μου οὕτως· | "ὃν τρόπον σήμερον
πῶ|λος βασιλεῖ χρήσιμος | διὰ τῆς δυνάμεως τῶν | (8)
ἱπποφόρβων γίνεται | βασιλέως ὄχημα, ἵν᾽ ἐν | τιμῆι καὶ
δόξηι ἐπικα|θεσθεὶς αὐτῶι τὸ ἴδιον | (12) [α]ὐτοῦ κατα-
πράξηται | [πρᾶγμα, το]ύτωι τῶι τρό|[πωι ὁ νοῦς ἔχει τ]ὸ̣
σῶμα, | [ἵνα ποιήσηι τὸ ἀγ]αθόν. | . . .

(15.1) . . . τ̣όπ̣ου ν[.....]. | [..π]ρὸς ἀνάπαυσιν τοῦ |
βασιλέως καὶ κατεκο|(4)σμήθη τι ἔνδυμα τῶι | ἐνδυσαμένωι·
κατε|σκευάσθη μὲν ἡ ναῦς | τῶι ἀρίστωι κυβερνή|(8)τηι ἵνα
ἀγρεύσηι τὰ κει|μήλια ἐκ τῆς θαλάσσης· | ἐκτίσθη δὲ τὸ
ἱερὸν πρὸς | εὔκλειαν τοῦ νοῦ καὶ | (12) ὁ ἁγιώτατος μὲν
νεώς | πρὸς ἀποκάλυψιν τῆς | αὐτοῦ σοφίας· πεπλή|ρωται δ᾽
ὁ [..... ....] | (16) τόκο[ς] . . .

(16.1) . . . ἐν σ[ώματι] | τοὺς ἀνδραποδισ[θέν]|τας ἀπὸ
τῶν δυναστῶ̣ν̣ | (4) καὶ λυτρώαιτο καὶ ἐ|λευθερώσηι τὰ
σφέτε|ρα μέλη ἐκ τῆς ὑποτα|γῆς τῶν στασιαστῶν | (8) καὶ
τῆς τῶν ἐπιτροπευ|όντων ἐξουσίας

same: "Strengthen your power, (12) make your mind strong, and submit to all that is about to come upon you." . . .

(14.1) ". . . we have been sent out by the great [fathers]."

Baraies the Teacher

(4) My lord (Mani) said thus: "Just as nowadays a young horse, used by a king, (8) becomes the king's mount through the capability of the horse trainers, so that he might sit upon it in honor and glory and (12) carry out his particular [task], in this same way [the mind possesses the] body, [in order to do the] good. . . .

(15.1) . . . of [. . .] place [. . .] for the king's rest; and (4) a certain garment was fitted for the one who put it on; the ship was equipped for the best skipper (8) so that he might catch valued treasures from the sea; the holy place was set up for glory of the mind; and (12) the most holy shrine, for revelation of its wisdom; the [. . .] interest [. . .] has been paid fully . . .

(16.1) . . . in (the) [body], (that) he might ransom those enslaved from the powers (of the other world) (4) and set free their members from the subjection of the rebels (8) and from the authority of those who keep

καὶ | δι᾿ αὐτοῦ μὲν φάνηι τῆς | ἰδίας γνώσεως τὴν
ἀ|(12)λήθειαν, ἐν αὐτῶι δὲ ἀ|ναπετάσηι τὴν θύραν | τοῖς
καθειργμένοις | [καὶ δι᾿ αὐτο]ῦ μὲν ὀρέξηι | (16) [τὴν
εὐζωίαν ἐ]κε[ί]νοις . . .

(17.1) . . . καὶ πάντων νό|μων, ἐλευθερώσηι δὲ | τὰς
ψυχὰς τῆς ἀγνοί|(4)ας γινόμενος παρά|κλητος καὶ κορυ-
φαῖος | τῆς κατὰ τήνδε τὴν | γενεὰν ἀποστολῆς. κα|(8)τὰ
τὸν καιρὸν τοίνυν | καθ᾿ ὃν συνεπεράνθη | μου τὸ σῶμα ἐν
τέλει, | παραχρῆμα καταπτὰς | (12) ὤφθη ἔμπροσθέν μου |
ἐκεῖνο τὸ εὐειδέστα|τον καὶ μέγιστον κά|τοπτρον τ[οῦ
προσώ]|(16)που μ[ου] . . .

(18.) . . . [ὅτε τεσσάρων καὶ εἴ]|(1)κοσι ἐτῶν ὑπῆρξα [ἐν] |
τῶι ἔτει ὧι ὑπέταξεν Ἄ|τραν τὴν πόλιν Δαριάρ|(4)δαξαρ
ὁ βασιλεὺς τῆς Περ|σίδος, ἐν ὧι καὶ Σαπώρης | ὁ βασιλεὺς
ὁ υἱὸς αὐτοῦ | διάδημα μέγιστον ἀνε|(8)δήσατο, κατὰ τὸν
μῆνα | τὸν Φαρμοῦθι ἐν τῆι η᾿ ἡ|μέραι τῆς σελήνης ὁ
μα|καριώτατος κύριος ἐσπλ[αγ]|(12)χνίσθη ἐπ᾿ ἐμὲ καὶ με
ἐκ[ά]|λεσεν εἰς τὴν αὐτοῦ χά|ριν καὶ ἀπέστειλέν μοι |
[ἐκεῖθεν ε]ὐθὺς σύζυγόν | (16) [μου τὸν ἐν δόξηι
μ]εγάληι | [φαινόμενον] . . .

(19.2) . . . [ὁ] μνήστωρ καὶ μη[νυτὴς] | πασῶν ἀρίστων
συμβο[υ]|(4)λιῶν τῶν ἐκ τοῦ πατρὸς τοῦ | ἡμετέρου καὶ τῆς

guard, and through it (i.e., the body) he might disclose
the truth of its own knowledge, (12) and in it open wide
the door to those confined within, [and through it] he
might hold out (16) [well-being] to those . . .

(17.1) . . . and from all laws, and (that) he might free
the souls from ignorance (4) by becoming paraclete and
leader of the apostleship in this generation. (8) Then,
at the time when my body reached its full growth,
immediately there flew down and (12) appeared before me
that most beautiful and greatest mirror-image of [my
self] . . .

(18.1) . . . [When] I was twenty[-four] years old, [in]
the year in which Dariardaxar, (4) the King of Persia,
subdued the city Atra, also in which his son Sapores, the
King, crowned himself with the grand diadem, (8) in the
month of Pharmouthi, on the eighth day of the lunar month,
the most blessed Lord was greatly moved with compassion
(12) for me, called me into his grace, and immediately
sent to me [from there my] Twin, (16) [appearing in]
great [glory] . . .

(19.2) . . . [he] (is) mindful of and informer of all the
best counsels (4) from our Father and from the good first

ἀπο|πρὸ πρώτης δεξιᾶς ἀγα|θῆς."

    καὶ πάλιν εἶπεν οὕ|(8)τως ὡς "ὁπηνίκα ηὐδό|κησεν ὁ
πατήρ μου καὶ πε|ποίηται ἐπ᾽ ἐμὲ ἔλεόν | τε καὶ οἶκτον εἰς
τὸ λυ|(12)τρώσασθαι ἐκ τῆς τῶν | δογματιστῶν πλάνης, |
ποιήσας ἐπ᾽ ἐμὲ τὴν φει|δὼ διὰ τῶν πλείστων | (16) αὐτοῦ
φα[νερώσεων] ἀπ[έ]|στειλέ[ν μοι τὸν σύζυ]|γό[ν μου] . . .

(20.1) . . . [ἀ]ρ[ίσ]τ[ην ἐλπίδα] | [καὶ] ἀπολύτρωσιν
τλ[η]|[τ]ικοῖς καὶ τὰς ἀληθεστά|(4)τας ὑποθήκας τε καὶ
γνώ|μας καὶ τὴν ἐκ τοῦ ἡμε|τέρου πατρὸς χειροθεσίαν. |
ὁπηνίκα τοίνυν ἀφῖκται, | (8) διελύσατό με καὶ διώρι|σε
καὶ ἀπεσπάσατο ἐκ μέ|σου τοῦ νόμου ἐκείνου | καθ᾽ ὃν
ἀνετράφην. κατὰ | (12) τοῦτον τὸν τρόπον ἐ|κάλεσέν με
καὶ ἐπελέξα|το καὶ εἵλκυσεν καὶ διέ|στησεν ἐκ μέσου
τού|(16)τ[ων. ....]ε[λ]κύσας δέ | [με εἰς θείαν π]λευρὰν |
. . .

(21.2) ⁶. . . καὶ τίς εἰμι καὶ | τοὐμὸν σῶμα καὶ ποίωι |
(4) τρόπωι ἐλήλυθα καὶ ὡς | γέγονεν ἡ ἄφιξίς μου | εἰς
τόνδε τὸν κόσμον | καὶ τίς γίγνομαι τῶν ὑ|(8)παρχόντων
κατὰ τὴν | ὑπεροχὴν ἐπισημοτά|των καὶ ὡς ἐγεννήθην |
εἰς τὸ σαρκῶδες τοῦτο | (12) σῶμα ἢ διὰ ποίαν μαι|ευθεὶς
ἐλοχεύθην κατὰ | τὴν σάρκα ταύτην καὶ | ἀπὸ τίνος
ἔρ[ω]τι κατε|(16)σπάρην . . .

right hand far away."

And again, he (Mani) spoke thus: (8) "When my
Father was pleased and had mercy and compassion on me, to
(12) ransom (me) from the error of the Sectarians, he
took consideration of me through his very many (16) [reve-
lations], (and) he sent [to me] my [Twin] . . .

(20.1) . . . [best hope and] redemption for (those who)
suffer patiently, the truest (4) instructions and
counsels, and the laying on of hands from our Father.
When, then, he (the Twin) came, (8) he delivered,
separated, and pulled me away from the midst of that Law
in which I was reared. In (12) this way he called, chose,
drew, and severed me from their midst [. . .], (16)
drawing [me to the divine] side. . . .

(21.2) (the Twin is instructing Mani concerning)[6] . . .
who I am, what my body is, in what (4) way I have come,
how my arrival into this world took place, who I am of the
(8) ones most renowned for their eminence, how I was
begotten into this fleshly (12) body, by what woman I was
delivered and born according to the flesh, and by whose
[passion] (16) I was engendered . . .

---

[6]The main verb of an extended indirect discourse is
lost.

22

(22.1) . . . καὶ πῶς [.......] | γμα γεγένηται·[7] κα[ὶ ὁ] |
πατήρ μου ὁ ἐν ὕψει τίς τ[υγ] | (4) χάνει ἢ ποίωι τρόπωι
δι | αστὰς αὐτοῦ ἀπεστάλην | κατὰ τὴν αὐτοῦ γνώ | μην καὶ
ποίαν ἐντολήν | (8) τε καὶ ὑποθήκην δεδώ | ρηταί μοι πρὶν
ἐνδύσω | μαι τὸ ὄργανον τόδε καὶ | πρὶν πλανηθῶ ἐν τῆι |
(12) σαρκὶ ταύτηι τῆι βδελυ | ρώδει καὶ πρὶν ἐνδῦναί | με
τήν τε μέθην αὐτῆς | καὶ τὸν τρόπον, καὶ ὅστις |
(16) [ἐκεῖνός ἐστι]ν αὐτὸς σύ | [ζυγός μου ἄγρυ]πνος ὤν . . .

(23.1) . . . [τ]ὰ ἀπόρρητα καὶ τὰ | [θεά]ματα καὶ τὰς
ὑπερβο | λὰς τοὐμοῦ πατρός, καὶ περὶ | (4) ἐμοῦ τίς
τυγχάνω ὤν, | καὶ ὁ σύζυγός μου ὁ ἀρα | ρὼς τίς ποτ᾽
ἐστίν. | ἔτι δὲ καὶ περὶ τῆς ψυχῆς | (8) μου, ἥτις
πάντων τῶν | κόσμων ὑπάρχει ψυ | χή, ἢ τίς καὶ αὐτή ἐστιν |
ἢ γέγονε πῶς. ἔφηνε | (12) δ᾽ αὖ ἐμοὶ πρὸς τούτοις | τά
τε ἄπειρα ὕψη καὶ τὰ | βάθη τὰ ἀνεξιχνίαστα, | ὑπέδειξέ[ν
μοι] πάντ[α] | . . .

(22.1) . . . and how [. . .] came into being;[7] and who my

Father on high is; (4) or in what way, severed from him,

I was sent out according to his purpose; and what sort of

commission (8) and counsel he has given to me before I

clothed myself in this instrument, and before I was led

astray in (12) this detestable flesh, and before I

clothed myself with its drunkenness and habits; and who

(16) [that one is, who] is himself [my ever-vigilant

Twin] . . .

(23.1) (the Twin showed Mani) . . . the secrets and

[visions] and the perfections of my Father; and concerning

(4) me, who I am, and who my inseparable Twin is; more-

over, concerning my soul, (8) which exists as the soul of

all the worlds, both what it itself is and how it came to

be. (12) Beside these, he revealed to me the boundless

heights and the unfathomable depths; he showed [me] all

. . .

---

[7]Translators read, with the critical text: καὶ πῶς
[..... ...]|γμα γεγένηται.

(24.3)   ε̣ὐ̣σ̣εβ[ῶς ..... .] | (4) τε αὐτὸν

καὶ ἐκτησά|μην ὡς ἴδιον κτῆμα. |

ἐπίστευσα δ᾽ αὐτὸν

ἐμὸν | ὑπάρχοντά τε καὶ ὄν|(8)τα

καὶ σύμβουλον ἀγα|θὸν καὶ χρηστὸν ὄντα. |

ἐπέγνων μὲν αὐτὸν

καὶ | συνῆκα ὅτι ἐκεῖνος ἐ|(12)γὼ εἰμι

ἐξ οὗ διεκρίθην. |

ἐπεμαρτύρησα δὲ

ὅτι ἐ|γὼ ἐκε[ῖ]νος αὐτός εἰμι |

ἀ̣κ̣λ̣ο̣ν̣[ητο]ς̣ ὑπάρχων. | . . ."

(25.1) . . . ἔλεγεν δ᾽ αὖ | [πάλιν] οὕτως ὡς "σὺν πλεί|στ̣η̣ι̣

μηχανῆι καὶ ἐπιστή|(4)μηι περιῆλθον ἐν ἐκείνωι | τῶι

νόμωι διαφυλάττων | τήνδε τὴν ἐλπίδα ἐν | φρονήσει τῆι

ἐμαυτοῦ | (8) μηδενὸς αἰσθομένου | τίς ποτ᾽ ἐστὶν τὸ

παρ᾽ ἐμ[οὶ] | ὄν· καὶ αὐτὸς ἐγὼ ἀπεκά|λυψα οὐδενὶ οὐδὲν

κ[α]|(12)τὰ τὸν χρόνον ἐκεῖνον | πλεῖστον ὑπάρχοντ̣α̣. |

ἀλλ᾽ οὐδὲ ἐκείνοις π[αρα]|πλήσια τ̣ὸ̣ ἔ̣θ̣ι̣μ̣ο̣ν̣ [ἔσχον]|

(16) τὸ σαρκῶ[δε]ς̣ . . .

(26.) . . . [οὐδὲν ἀπεκάλυ]|(1)ψα τῶν γενομένων οὐ|δὲ

τῶν γενησομένων | οὐδ᾽ ὅτι ἐστὶν ὃ ἔγνων | (4) ἢ τί

τυγχάνει ὃ προσε|δεξάμην." |

οἱ διδάσκαλοι λέγουσιν |

Ὁπηνίκα τοίνυν τὰ ἀπόρ|(8)ρητα ταῦτα καὶ μέγιστα |

ἐξέφηνέ μοι ἐκεῖνος ὁ | πανευκλεὴς καὶ πανευ|δ̣αίμων,

(24.3)   . . . reverently [. . .] (4)

    and I acquired him as my own possession.

I believed

    that he belongs to me and (8) is (mine)

    and is a good and excellent counselor.

I recognized him

    and understood that (12) I am that one

    from whom I was separated.

I testified

    that I myself am that one

    who is unshakable. . . ."

(25.1) . . . And [again] he (Mani) said thus: "With the greatest possible ingenuity and skill (4) I went about in that Law, preserving this hope in my heart; (8) no one perceived who it was that was with me, and I myself revealed nothing to anyone during (12) that great period of time. But neither [did I], like them, [keep] the fleshly custom . . .

(26.1) I [revealed nothing] of what happened, or of what will happen, nor what it is that I knew, (4) or what it is that I had received."

               The Teachers Say

    When, then, (8) that all-glorious and all-blessed one (the Twin) disclosed to me these exceedingly great

ἤρξατο λέγειν | (12) [πρ]ός με· "τόδε τὸ μυστή|[ριον]
ἀπεκάλ[υ]ψά σοι [. . .] (15) [ἀπο]καλύψαι[7a] . . ."

(pp. 27 and 28 are missing)

(29.1) τῆς ἀποτε[μ]νούσης ζ[ιζά]|νια καὶ καρποὺς τῆς γῆς |
ἐκτεμεῖν τοὺς ἀκρεμό|(4)νας πάντων τῶν στας[ι]|αστῶν,
αὐτῆς μόνης ὁ[ο]|ξαζομένης τῆς ἀλη[θεί]|ας καὶ βασι-
λευούση[ς πα]|(8)ραπλησί[ω]ς τῶι .[. . . . . ὕ]|ψους . . .

(30.1) [. . . . ἐ]κείνοις τοῖς κατὰ | σ[ά]ρκα συνημμένοις·
ἀλ|λὰ καὶ τοῦτον τὸν τρό|(4)πον κατὰ βραχὺ βραχὺ |
[ἐ]μαυτὸν διώρισα ἐκ μέ|[σο]υ τοῦ νόμου ἐκείνου |
[καθ'] ὃν ἀνετράφην, ὑπερ|(8)[μέτ]ρως θα[υ]μάζων
ἐ|[κεῖνα . . .] μυστή|[ρια . . . π]λῆθος[8] . . .

(31.1) πλήθει, μονήρης δ' ἐγώ· | πλουτεῖ μὲν γὰρ ταῦτα, |
πένομαι δ' ἐγώ· πῶς τοί|(4)νυν μόνος ὢν παρὰ πάν|τας
οἷος ἔσομαι τὸ μυ|στήριον τοῦτο ἀποκα|λύψαι ἐν μέσωι
τοῦ [πλ]ή|(8)θους τοῦ ἐ[νεχομένου ἐν] | πλάνηι; . . .

secrets, he began to say (12) to me: "This mystery I have revealed to you [. . .] to reveal[7a] . . ."

(pages 27 and 28 are missing)

(29.1) while it cuts away the weeds and the fruits of the earth to cut off the branches (4) of all the rebels, (thus) it is truth that alone is glorified and reigns (8) like the [. . .] of Height . . .

(30.1) to those bound together according to the flesh; but also in this way, (4) little by little, I detached myself from the midst of that Law [in] which I was reared, (8) marveling beyond all measure at [those] mysteries [. . .] many[8] . . .

(31.1) in number, but I am solitary. For these are rich, but I am poor. How then (4) shall I, alone against all, be able to reveal this mystery in the midst of the multitude (8) [entangled in] error? . . .

[7a]Translators read, with the critical text: [ἀπο]καλύψαι.

[8]Translators read, with the critical text: π]λῆθος.

(32.1) σθηναι· δι καὶ σύνεισιν | πλεῖστοι βοηθοί. | ἐμοῦ
δὲ ταῦτα λογιζο| (4)μένου καὶ σκεπτομέ|νου κατὰ τὴν
φρένα, | αὐτόθι ἀνέσχεν καταν|τ[ι]κρὺ ἐμοῦ στὰς ὁ
ἐν| (8) [δοξότατ]ός μου σύζυ|[γος λέγων πρ]ὸς ἐμέ· |
"[. . . σοι ἀπο]καλυφθῆ| (14) [σομαι ὡς ἀγαθ]ὸς σύμβου|[λος
πασῶν τῶν σ]υμβου| (16) [λειῶν· καὶ νῦν τ]υγχάνω | [.....
πάντων σ]ου βουλη|[μάτων ...... σύ]μβουλος· | . . .
εὔτρε| (20) [πῆς ...... ἀποκαλ]υφθῆ|[σομαι] . . .

(33.1) καὶ δι' αὐτὸ τοῦτο ἐγεν|νήθης. σὺ τοίνυν πάν|τα
ἅπερ ἔδωκά σοι ἐξη| (4)γοῦ. ἐγὼ δὲ ἐπίκουρός | σου καὶ
φύλαξ ἔσομαι | κατὰ πάντα καιρόν." |

                    Τιμόθεος |

. . .

(34.1) τοῦ φωτὸς πατέρων. | καὶ πάντα τὰ γιγνόμε|να ἐν
τοῖς πλοίοις ἀπεκά| (4)λυπτέ μοι. | ἀνέπτυξε δ' αὖ πάλιν
τὸν | κόλπον τοῦ κίονος, καὶ | τοὺς πατέρας καὶ τὰ
σθέ| (8)νη τὰ ἀλκιμώτατα | [τὰ ἁ]ποκρυπτόμενα . . .

(35.) . . .[-θεῖ]| (1)σα ἐκλεγῆναι καὶ ὀφθῆ|ναί μοι,
παρασκευασθεῖ|σα καὶ τελειουργηθεῖσα | (4) ἔν τε τοῖς
διδασκάλοις | αὐτῆς καὶ ἐπισκόποις, | ἐκλεκτοῖς τε καὶ
κατη|χουμένοις, ἔν τε τρα| (8)πέζαις εὐσεβεία{ι}ς καὶ |
βοηθοῖς μεγίστοι[ς] καὶ | πᾶσι τοῖς μέλ[λουσι γί]|γνεσθαι

. . .

(32.1) with which also there are associated very many helpers. Now while I was considering (4) and pondering these things in my heart, immediately (8) my [most glorious] Twin appeared, standing directly opposite to me, [saying] to me: "[. . . to you I shall be] revealed (14) [as a good] counselor [of all] counsels. (16) [And now] I am [. . . of all your] plans [. . .] counselor. [. . .] ready (20) [. . . I shall be] revealed . . .

(33.1) and for this very thing you were begotten. You, then, expound all that I have given to you. (4) I shall be your ally and protector at all times."

Timothy

. . .

(34.1) of the Fathers of Light. All that occurs in the ships he revealed (4) to me. And again, he disclosed the womb of the pillar, the Fathers, and the (8) mightiest powers [which are] hidden . . .

(35.1) to be chosen and appear to me; prepared and perfected (4) with its teachers and bishops, elect and catechumens, with the (8) dining tables <of> piety and greatest helpers, and all who are about to become . . .

30

(36.) . . . [κρυπ]|(1)τὰς καὶ ἀπορρήτους ἀπε|κάλυψέν

μοι, πρόσθεν | αὐτοῦ προσκυνήσας | (4) εἶπον· "ταῦτα ἅπερ

αἰ|τοῦμαι παρὰ σοῦ, δίδον|ταί μοι καὶ συμπαρα|μενοῦσίν

μοι κατὰ πάν|(8)τα καιρὸν μὴ ἀποκρυ|πτόμενα ἀλλὰ

προ|[δήλω]ς διὰ τῶν χει|[ρῶν μου φαι]νόμενα | (12) [.....

.... πᾶ]σιν ὀφθαλ|[μοῖς] . . .

(37.) . . . [παρα]|(1)πέμψωμαι τοῖς πλημ|μελέσι· καὶ

πάλιν κα|τὰ τὴν σοφίαν μηδεὶς | (4) με νικήσῃ· καὶ ἵνα

ὦ | ἄνοσος καὶ ἀκίνδυνος· | καὶ ὅπως αἱ ψυχαὶ τῶν |

νικητῶν ἐξερχόμε|(8)ναι ἀπὸ τοῦ κόσμου πᾶ|σιν ὀφθαλμοῖς

ἀνθρώπων | θεωρηθῶσιν· | ὁμοίω[ς] . . .

(38.) κ[αὶ πάλιν, ὅταν περιλημ]|(1)φθῶ ὑπὸ θλίψεως

ἢ δι|ωγμῶν, ἀποκρυβῶ ἀπ' ἔμ|προσθεν τῶν ἐχθρῶν |

(4) μου." |

    τότε ὁ ἐνδοξότατος ἐ|κεῖνος εἶπεν πρὸς ἐμέ· | "τὰς

δωρεὰς ταύτας | (8) ἅσπερ ἠτήσω παρ' ἐμοῦ, | τισὶ μὲν

μία ἐξ αὐτῶν | [δίδο]ται τοῖς ἀδελφοῖς | [καὶ ταῖς

ἀδελφ]αῖς τοῖς κα|(12)[τὰ] . . .

(39.1) πρὸς τὸ πρέπον τῆι γενε|ᾶι καθ' ἣν ἀπεκαλύφθης, |

συγγνώμην τῶν ἁμαρ|(4)τημάτων ὅπως παραπέμ|ψῃς τοῖς

ἁμαρτάνου|σιν ἐκείνοις τοῖς τὴν | μετάνοιαν ἐκ σοῦ

προσ|(8)δεχομένοις καὶ τῆι ὁσι|ότητι πειθομένοις,

(36.1) (when) he revealed to me (the) [hidden] and secret
(things), I fell down before him and (4) said: "These
things which I ask from you are given to me and will
remain with me at all (8) times, not hidden but [clearly]
manifested through [my] hands (12) [. . .] to [all] eyes
. . .

(37.1) (that) I might forgive those who err, and again,
(that) no one might get the better of me in wisdom,
(4) and that I may be healthy and free from danger. Also
that the souls of the victors (8) may be seen, coming out
from the world, by every human eye. Likewise . . .

(38.) [and again, when] I [am beset] (1) by affliction or persecutions, (that) I might be hidden from
before my enemies."

   (4) Then that most glorious one said to me: "These
gifts (8) which you asked of me, one of them [is given]
to some of the brothers [and the sisters], who (12)
[according to . . .]

(39.1) (the Twin continues speaking) as it befits the
generation in which you were revealed, (4) in order that
you might impart pardon of sins to those sinners who
accept repentance from you (8) and rely on holiness, so

32

ἵνα | λύσας παραπέ[μψηις ἄφεσιν] | πλημ[μελειῶν καί
ἐγ]|(12)κλήσ[εων σου τῆι ἐκλο]|γῆι. ἔτ[ι] . . .

(40.1) καί πάλιν εἴ ποτ᾽, ἂν θλιβῆις, | ἐπικαλέσηι με,
ἐγώ πλη|σίον σου εὑρεθήσομαι | (4) ἐστώς, ὑπερασπιστής |
σου ἐν πάσηι θλίψει καί | κινδύνωι γενησόμε|νος. τά δέ
σημεῖα ταῦτα | (8) ἅπερ με ᾐτήσω ἐν ἐμοί | γνωσθήσονται
ὡς καί | [ἀποκαλ]υφθῆναί σοι δη|[λότατα. ἀποδεί]ξ̲ω γάρ
. . .

(41.) . . . [τέρα]|(1)τα τοῦ ψεύδους τά ἀν|τισταθέντα
πρός αὐτούς. | διά γάρ τῶν σημείων τῆς | (4) ἀληθείας
κατηργήθη | τά τοῦ ψεύδους." |
    μετά δέ τό ταῦτα εἰπεῖν | πρός ἐμέ τόν ἔνδοξό|-
(8)τατον καί ἐνδυναμῶ|σαί με καί παραθαρσῦ|ναι πρός τήν
. . .

(42.1) καί λαβεῖν ἐξ αὐτῆς κλη|ματίδας πρός τό πληθῦ|ναι
τόν ταύτης γόνον, | (4) ἵν᾽ οὕτως ἀπό μιᾶς ἀμ|πέλου
τῆς ἀφ᾽ ἑνός σπέρ|ματος καλλίστου--εὐ|πορήσας μέντοι
γε γῆς | (8) ἀρίστης ἱκανῆς ἀνα|φῦναι ἐκείνην τήν |
[ἄμπελο]ν̲ καί δυναμέ|[νης ....].ε̲ι̲ν̲--ἐκ ταύ|(12)[της]
. . .

that you might set free and impart [forgiveness of]
trespasses [and (12) accusations to your Elect]. Still
. . .

(40.1) And again, if you ever are in affliction and call
upon me, I shall be found standing near you, (4) to be
your shield in every affliction and danger. These signs
(8) for which you asked me will be made known through me,
so that they may be revealed [most] clearly to you. For
I shall [show] . . .

(41.1) [wonders] of the lie which are pitted against
them. For it is through the signs of the (4) truth that
those of the lie are nullified."

Now after the most glorious one said these things to
me, (8) and strengthened and encouraged me regarding the
. . .

(42.1) and to take from it branches in order to increase
its growth, (4) so that thus from one vine, the one from
the singularly finest seed—so long as (the gardener) has
provided it with (8) choicest earth sufficient to grow
that [vine] and able to [. . .] —from this . . .

34

(43.1) τό τε ὕψος καὶ τὸ βάθος | καὶ τὴν ἀνάπαυσιν καὶ |
τὴν κόλασιν. ἀπεκά|(4)λυψε δέ μοι μυστήρια | τὰ λεληθότα
τὸν κό|σμον ἃ οὐκ ἐξὸν ἰδεῖν | πάντα ἄνθρωπον οὐδὲ
ἀκοῦσαι. |

(8) ὅτε τοίνυν ἐξηραύνη|σα πάντα τὰ θεωρηθέν|τα
μοι ἐν τ[..... .....] | αὐτοῦ . . .

(44.1) ται· μὴ πᾶσι διδόμενα, | τότε παραχρῆμα διεῖ|λον
ἐμαυτὸν ἀπὸ τῶν | (4) τάξεων ἐκείνου τοῦ | δόγματος καθ᾽
ὃ ἀνετρά|φην, καὶ γέγονα παρα|πλήσιος ὀθνείωι καὶ
μο|(8)νήρει ἐν μέσωι αὐτῶν | μέχρι φθάσαι τὸν και|[ρὸν
τοῦ ἀπο]βῆναί με ἀ|[π᾽ ἐκείνου τ]οῦ δόγμα|(12)[τος] . . .

(19-20) [Βαραίης ὁ διδάσκαλος][9]

. . .

(45.1) γνῶτε τοίνυν, ὦ ἀδελφοί, | καὶ σύνετε πάντα ταῦ|τα
τὰ ἐνθάδε γραφέντα, | (4) καὶ περὶ τοῦ τρόπου κα|θ᾽ ὃν
ἀπεστάλη ἥδε ἡ ἀπο|στολὴ ἡ κατὰ τήνδε | τὴν γενεὰν καθὼς
ἐδι|(8)δάχθημεν παρ᾽ αὐτοῦ, | ἔτι δὲ καὶ περὶ τοῦ
[σώ]|ματος [αὐτοῦ] . . .

(43.1) the Height and the Depth, the Rest and the
Chastisement. (4) Now he revealed to me mysteries hidden
to the world, which are not permitted for anyone to see
or hear.

   (8) When, then, I examined everything beheld by me
in his [. . .] . . .

(44.1) which is not given to all. Then, immediately I
separated myself from the (4) ordinances of that teaching
in which I was reared, and became like a stranger and a
(8) solitary in their midst, until the time came for me
to depart from [that] teaching . . .

          (19-20) [Baraies the Teacher][9]
. . .

(45.1) Know, then, brothers, and understand all these
things written herein: (4) concerning the way in which
this apostleship in this generation was sent, just as
(8) we have been taught from him; and also concerning
[his] body . . .

---

[9]For the reconstruction: Cf. *ZPE* 19 (1975) 45 n. 80.

(46.1) τῆς ἀποστολῆς ταύτης | τοῦ πνεύματος τοῦ
παρακλή|του καὶ μεταβληθείς[10] | (4) εἴπηι ὅτι "οὗτοι
μόνοι γε|γράφασιν ἁρπαγὴν τοῦ | διδασκάλου αὐτῶν | πρὸς
καύχησιν." | (8) πάλιν δὲ καὶ περὶ τῆς γέν|[νη]ς τοῦ
σώματος αὐτοῦ[11] . . .

(47.1) ἁμαρτάνει. ὁ γάρ τοι βου|λόμενος ἀκουέτω καὶ |
προσεχέτω ὡς εἷς ἕκα|(4)στος τῶν προγενεστέ|ρων
πατέρων τὴν ἰ|δίαν ἀποκάλυψιν ἔδει|ξεν τῆι ἑαυτοῦ
ἐκλογῆι, | (8) ἣν ἐξελέξατο καὶ συνή|γαγεν κατ᾽ ἐκείνην |
τὴν γενεὰν καθ᾽ ἣν ἐ|φάνη, καὶ γράψας κα|(12)τέλειψεν
τοῖς μετα|γενεστέροις. καὶ ὁ μὲν | περὶ ἁρπαγῆς αὐτοῦ |
ἐδήλω[σ]εν, οἱ δὲ ἔξω | (16) ὡμίλ[η]σαν . . .

(48.1) γράψαι καὶ ἀποδεῖξαι | μετέπειτα καὶ ἐγκω|μιάσαι
καὶ μεγαλῦναι | (4) τοὺς διδασκάλους ἑαυ|τῶν καὶ
τὴν ἀλήθειαν | καὶ τὴν ἐλπίδα τὴν ἀ|ποκαλυφθεῖσαν
αὐτοῖς. | (8) οὕτω τοίνυν εἷς ἕκαστος | κατὰ τὴν περίοδον
καὶ | περιφορὰν τῆς ἀποστο|λῆς αὐτοῦ ὡς ἐθεώρη|(12)σεν
εἶπεν καὶ γέγραφεν | πρὸς ὑπομνηματισμόν-- | ἔτι δὲ καὶ
περὶ τῆς ἁρ|παγῆς αὐτοῦ. |
     (16) [οὕτ]ω πρῶτο[ς ὁ] Αδαμ | [. . . . . .].ωτ[..]
εἶπεν | [ἐν τῆι ἀποκαλύψει] αὐτοῦ· | "[. . . ἄγ]γελον[11a] |
. . .

(46.1) (concerning) this apostleship of the Spirit, the Paraclete, (so that no one) will change allegiance[10] (4) and say: "These alone have written about the rapture of their teacher in order to boast." (8) And again, concerning the origin of his body[11] . . .

(47.1) he sins. For let the one who is willing hear and pay attention, how each one (4) of the forefathers showed his own revelation to his elect, (8) which he chose and brought together in that generation in which he appeared, and how he wrote (it) and (12) bequeathed (it) to posterity. Now he (i.e., each forefather) explained about his rapture; and they (i.e., the elect) (16) preached it to outsiders . . .

(48.1) to write and demonstrate hereafter and to praise and extol (4) their teachers and the truth and the hope which was revealed to them. (8) So, then, during the course and circuit of his apostleship each one, as he saw, (12) spoke and wrote for a memoir--as well as about his rapture.

(16) [Thus] first Adam [. . .] said [in] his [Apocalypse]: "[. . .] angel[11a] . . .

---

[10]Μεταβληθείς refers to a changing from, or a desertion of, community practices: Cf. *ZPE* 19 (1975) 47 n. 84.

[11]Source of the title of the Codex?

[11a]Translators read, with the critical text: ἄγ]γελον.

(49.) . . . [λαμ] | (1)προῦ προσώπου σου ὃν ἐ|γὼ οὐ γινώσκω."
τότε | ἔφη αὐτῶι· "ἐγώ εἰμι Βάλ|(4)σαμος ὁ μέγιστος
ἄγγε|λος τοῦ φωτός· ὅθεν δε|ξάμενος γράψον ταῦτα | ἅπερ
σοι ἀποκαλύπτω ἐν | (8) χάρτηι καθαρωτάτωι καὶ | μὴ
φθειρομένωι καὶ σῆ|τα μὴ ἐπιδεχομένωι"--χω|ρὶς καὶ ἄλλων
πλείστων | (12) ὧν αὐτῶι ἀπεκάλυψεν | ἐν τῆι ὀπτασίαι.
μεγίστη | γὰρ ἦν ἡ περὶ αὐτὸν δόξα. | ἐθεώρησεν δὲ κα[ὶ
τοὺς] | (16) ἀγγέλους κα[ὶ ἀρχιστρα]|τηγοὺ[ς καὶ
δυνάμεις] | μεγί[στας] . . .

(50.1) ον ὁ Αδαμ. καὶ γέγονεν | ὑπέρτερος παρὰ πάσας |
τὰς δυνάμεις καὶ τοὺς | (4) ἀγγέλους τῆς κτίσεως. | πολλὰ
δὲ καὶ ἄλλα τούτοις | παραπλήσια ὑπάρχει ἐν | ταῖς
γραφαῖς αὐτοῦ. |

(8) ὁμοίως δὲ καὶ Σηθηλ ὁ υ|ἱὸς αὐτοῦ οὕτω γέγρα|φεν
ἐν τῆι ἀποκαλύψει | αὐτοῦ λέγων ὅτι "ἤνοι|(12)ξα τοὺς
ὀφθαλμούς μου | καὶ ἐθεώρησα ἔμπροσ|θεν τοῦ προσώπου μου |
[ἄγγε]λον οὗ οὐκ ἠδυνά|(16)[μην τῆι πε]ίραι φῆσαι τὸ |
[φέγγος· οὐ γὰρ ἄ]λλο τι ὑ|[πῆρξεν ἀλλ' ἢ ἀστ]ραπαὶ . . .

(51.) . . . [ὁπη] | (1)νίκα τούτων ἠκροασά|μην, ἐχάρη μου
ἡ καρδί|α καὶ μετετράπη ἡ φρό|(4)νησις καὶ ἐγενόμην ὡς |
εἷς τῶν μεγίστων ἀγ|γέλων. ἐκεῖνος ὁ ἄγγελος | τὴν χεῖρα
αὐτοῦ ἐπὶ τὴν | (8) δεξιάν μου θεὶς καὶ ἐξέω|σέ με ἀπὸ
τοῦ κόσμου

(49.1) of the [radiant] face of you whom I do not know."
Then he said to him: "I am (4) Balsamos, the greatest
angel of light. Wherefore take and write these things
which I reveal to you on (8) most pure papyrus, incor-
ruptible and insusceptible to worms"--and he revealed to
him very many other things (12) in the vision as well.
For very great was the glory about him. Now he (Adam)
beheld also [the] (16) angels, [commanders-in-chief],
very great [powers] . . .

(50.1) Adam. And he became mightier than all the powers
and the (4) angels of creation. Now many other things
like these are in his writings.

(8) Likewise, also Sethel, his son, has written thus
in his Apocalypse, saying: "I opened (12) my eyes and
beheld before my face [an angel], whose (16) [splendor I]
was not able to speak of [from my experience. For it was
nothing] other [than] flashes of lightning . . .

(51.1) when I listened to these things, my heart
rejoiced and my mind was changed, (4) and I became like
one of the greatest angels. When that angel placed his
hand on (8) my right hand, he wrenched me from the world

ἐ|ξ οὗ ἐγεννήθην καὶ ἀπή|νεγκεν εἰς ἕτερον τό|(12)πον

πάνυ μέγιστον. | ἤκουον δὲ ἐκ τῶν ὄπιϑέν | μου ϑορύβου

μεγίστου | ἐκ τῶν ἀγγέλων ἐκεί|(16)νων ὃν κα[τέ]λειψ[α

ἐν] | τῶι κόσμ[ωι τούτωι ὑπαρ]|χόντων [καὶ .....

....]|των. εἶδ[ον δὲ ..... ἀν]|(20)ϑρώ[πους] . . .

(52.) π[ολλὰ δὲ τούτοις παρα]|(1)πλήσια ἐλέχϑη ἐν ταῖς |

γραφαῖς αὐτοῦ, καὶ ὡς | ἡρπάγη ὑπ᾽ ἐκείνου τοῦ |

(4) ἀγγέλου ἀπὸ κόσμου εἰς | κόσμον καὶ ἀπεκάλυψεν |

αὐτῶι μέγιστα μυστή|ρια τῆς μεγαλωσύνης. |

(8) πάλιν ἐν τῆι ἀποκαλύψει | τοῦ Ενως οὕτως λέγει· |

"ἐν τῶι τρίτωι ἔτει καὶ | ἐν τῶι μηνὶ τῶι δεκάτωι |

(12) ἐξῆλϑον εἰς περίπατον | εἰς τὴν γῆν τῆς ἐρήμου |

λογιζόμενος κατὰ τὴν | φρόνησιν περί τε τοῦ | (16)

[οὔ]ρα̣ν[ο]ῦ̣ καὶ τῆς γῆς καὶ | [περὶ πάντω]ν τῶν ἔργων |

[καὶ πραγμάτω]ν ποίωι λό|[γωι πεφύκασι] καὶ τῆι

τί|(20)[νος βουλήσει γεγό]ν̣ασιν . . .

(53.) . . . [ϑ]α|(1)νάτου καὶ ἥρπασεν σὺν | μεγίστηι

ἡσυχίαι. ἡ δὲ καρ|δία μου ἐβαρεῖτο, ἑτρό|(4)μησεν δὲ καὶ

τὰ μέλη | μου πάντα· καὶ οἱ σφόν|δυλοι τοῦ νώτου μου |

ἐκινήϑησαν πρὸς τῆς | (8) σφοδρότητος, καὶ οἱ πό|δες μου

ἐπὶ τοὺς ἀστρα|γάλους οὐχ εἱστήκεισαν. | ἀπῆλϑον δὲ εἰς

συχνὰς | (12) πεδιάδας καὶ εἶδον ἐκεῖ | ὄρη ὑψηλότατα. καὶ

ἥρ|πασε δέ με τὸ πνεῦμα καὶ ἀνή|νεγκέ με εἰς τὸ ὄρος ἐν |

(16) δυνάμει ἡσύχωι. κἀκεῖ | μοι ἀπεκ[αλύ]φ[ϑησαν πολ]|λαὶ

καὶ μεγ[άλαι ὄψεις.]" | πάλιν εἶ[πεν ὅτι "ὁ ἄγγε]|(20)λος

. . .

from which I was born and carried me off to another (12)
place exceedingly' great. Now I heard behind me a very
great uproar from those angels (16) whom I left behind
[in this] world [and . . .]. [And I] saw [. . . (20)
human] . . ."

(52.) [Now many things] like [these] (1) were mentioned
in his writings, how he was snatched up by that (4) angel
from world to world and (how) he revealed to him very
great mysteries of majesty.

(8) Again in the Apocalypse of Enosh it reads thus:
"In the third year, on the tenth month, (12) I went out
for a walk into the desert land, reflecting in my mind
about (16) heaven and earth and [about all] the works and
[things]--by what reason [they have come into being] and
by whose (20) [will] they exist. . . .

(53.1) of death and he snatched me up with very great
silence. My heart became heavy, (4) all my limbs
trembled, my backbone was shaken (8) violently, and my
feet did not stand on their pins. I went away to many
flat (12) plains and saw there extremely high mountains.
The Spirit snatched me up and carried me off to the
mountain in (16) silent power. There many great
[visions] were revealed to me." Again [he said . . .:
"The angel] . . .

42

(54.) ... [εἰς τὸ ἀρ]|(1)κτῶιον καὶ ἐθεώρησα ἐ|κεῖσε ὄρη
ὑπερμεγέθη | καὶ ἀγγέλους καὶ τόπους | (4) πολλούς. διε-
λάλησεν δέ | μοι καὶ εἶπεν· 'ὁ ἰσχυρότα|τος τὴν ὑπεροχὴν
ἀπέ|στειλέ με πρὸς σέ, ἵνα σοι | (8) ἀποκαλύψω τὰ
ἀπόρρη|τα ἃ ἐνεθυμήθης, ἐπει|δήπερ ἐξελέγης εἰς τὴν |
ἀλήθειαν. ταῦτα δὲ | (12) πάντα τὰ ἀπόκρυφα | γράψον ἐπὶ
πτύχας χαλ|κᾶς καὶ ἀπόθου ἐν τῆι γῆι | τῆς ἐρήμου. πάντα
δὲ | (16) ἃ γράφεις προδηλότα|[τα γρά]ψον· ἑτοίμως γὰρ |
[ἔχει ἡ ἀποκάλ]υψις αὖ|[τη ἡ ἐμή, ἣ οὔ] τελευτᾶι | (20)
[εἰς τὸν αἰῶνα, ἀπο]καλυ|[φθῆναι τοῖς ἀδελ]φοῖς | [καὶ ταῖς
ἀδελφαῖ]ς πᾶ|[σι.'" πολλὰ δὲ ἄλλα ὑ]πάρ|(55.1)χει τούτοις
ἐοικότα ἐν ταῖς | γραφαῖς αὐτοῦ ὑποδεικνύ|οντα περὶ τῆς
αὐτοῦ ἁρπα|(4)γῆς καὶ ἀποκαλύψεως. | πάντα γὰρ ἃ ἤκουσεν
καὶ | εἶδεν γράψας κατέλει|ψεν τοῖς μεταγενεστέ|(8)ροις
πᾶσι τοῦ τῆς ἀληθεί|ας πνεύματος. |

ὁμοίως δὲ καὶ ὁ Σημ τοῦ|τον τὸν τρόπον ἔφη ἐν | (12) τῆι
ἀποκαλύψει αὐτοῦ· | "ἐλογιζόμην περὶ πάντων | τῶν ἔργων
ποίωι τρό|πωι ἐγένοντο. ἐμοῦ δὲ | (16) διαλογιζομένου
ἐξα[ί]|φνης ἥρπ[ασέν] με π[νεῦμα τὸ] | ζῶν καὶ ἀν[ήνεγκεν
βί]|αι μεγίστη[ι καὶ με κατέ]|(20)στησεν κα[τὰ τὸ ἄκρον] |
ὄρους ὑψη[λοτάτου καὶ] | εἶπ[εν π]ρὸς [ἐμέ· '. . .]

(56.1) δόξαν δὸς τῶι μεγί|στωι τῆς τιμῆς βασι|λεῖ.'"
καὶ πάλιν εἶπεν | (4) ὅτι "σὺν ἡσυχίαι μὲν θύ|ραι ἀνεπε-
τάσθησαν, | διηιρέθησαν δὲ καὶ νε|φέλαι πρὸς τοῦ ἀνέ|(8)μου.
εἶδον δὲ καθεστή|ριον ἐπίδοξον ἀπὸ τοῦ | ὕψους τοῦ ἀνωτάτου |
κατερχόμενον καὶ | (12) μέγιστον ἄγγελον ἐ|φεστῶτα αὐτοῦ.

(54.1) [to the] north and I beheld there enormous mountains and angels and many places. (4) Now he spoke with
me and said: 'He who is eminently most powerful sent me
to you so that (8) I may reveal to you the secrets which
you pondered, since you were singled out for the truth.
Now all these things (12) that are hidden, write upon
bronze tablets and store them up in the desert land. All
(16) that you write, write most clearly. For this revelation [of mine, which never] dies, [is] ready (20) [to
be] revealed [to all the brothers and sisters.'" Now
many other things] (55.1) like these are in his writings,
which tell about his rapture (4) and revelation. For all
which he heard and saw he wrote down and bequeathed to
all posterity (8) of the Spirit of Truth.

Likewise, also, Shem spoke in this way in (12) his
Apocalypse: "I was reflecting about how all the works
came to be. As I (16) pondered, suddenly the living
[Spirit] snatched me, [lifted me up] with greatest
[force], set me [down] (20) on [the pinnacle] of a [very]
high mountain, [and] said to [me: '. . .]

(56.1) give glory to the greatest King of honor.'" And
again he said: (4) "Silently doors were thrown open and
clouds were parted by the wind. (8) I saw a glorious
throne room coming down from the highest height and a
(12) mighty angel standing by it.

44

ἡ δὲ | εἰκὼν τῆς ἰδέας τοῦ | προσώπου αὐτοῦ πε|(16)[ρ]ι-
καλλῆς καὶ ὡραία ἐτύγ|[χ]ανεν μᾶλλον τῆς στιλ|[βούσης
λα]μπηδόνος | [τοῦ ἡλί[ο]υ, ἔτι δὲ καὶ | (20) [τῆς
ἀστραπῆ]ς. . . .

(57.1) τῆς ποικιλίας στεφάνωι | πλακέντι ἐκ τῶν
Φαρ|μουθικῶν[12] ἀνθῶν. καὶ | (4) τότε ἡλλοιώθη ὁ χαρα|κτὴρ
τοῦ προσώπου μου | ὥστε καταπεσεῖν ἐπὶ τῆς | γῆς. καὶ οἱ
μὲν σφόνδυ|(8)λοι τοῦ νώτου μου διε|κλονήθησαν, οἱ δὲ
πόδες | μου οὐκ ἔστησαν ἐπὶ | τοὺς ἀστραγάλους.
πα|(12)ρέκυψεν δέ μοι φωνή | καλοῦσα ἀπὸ τοῦ καθε|στηρίου
καὶ ἐπελθοῦσά | μοι τῆς χειρὸς ἐλάβετο | (16) τῆς δεξιᾶς
καὶ ἀνέστη|σεν. φυσήσασα δὲ κατ[ὰ] | τῆς ὄψεώς μου
ἆσθμ[α] | ζωῆς προσθήκην [μοι] | (20) δυνάμεως εἰργά[σατο
καὶ] | δόξης."

    πλεῖσ[τα δὲ] | καὶ ἄλλα τούτ[ο]ι[ς παρα]|πλ[ήσια
ὑ]πάρ[χει ἐν ταῖς] | (58.1) αὐτοῦ γραφαῖς, καὶ τί|να
ἀπεκάλυψαν αὐτῶι οἱ | ἄγγελοι εἰπόντες γράψαι | (4) αὐτὰ
πρὸς ὑπομνημα | τισμόν. |

    πάλιν καὶ ὁ Ενωχ τοῦτον | τὸν τρόπον ἔφη ἐν τῆι |
(8) αὐτοῦ ἀποκαλύψει· "ἐγώ | εἰμι. Ενωχ ὁ δίκαιος· λύ|πη
μοί ἐστιν μεγάλη καὶ | χύσις δακρύων ἐκ τῶν | (12) ὀφ-
θαλμῶν μου διὰ τὸ | ἀκηκοέναι με τὸν ὀνει|δισμὸν τὸν
προελθόν|τα ἐκ στόματος τῶν ἀ|(16)[σ]εβῶν." ἔλεγεν δὲ |
[ὅ]τι "τῶν δακρύων ἐν | [τοῖ]ς ὀφθαλμοῖς μου ὄν|[των] καὶ
δεήσεως ἐν τῶι | (20) [στό]ματι ἐθεώρησα ἐπι|[στάν]τας
μοι ἀγγέλους ἐ|[πτὰ ἐκ το]ῦ οὐρανοῦ κα|[τερχομέ]νου[ς.

The image of the form of his face (16) was lovely and
fresh, more so than the gleaming splendor [of the sun],
still more so than (20) [lightning]. . . .

(57.1) of embroidery (like) a crown plaited with May[12]
flowers. (4) Then the features of my face were changed,
so that I fell upon the ground. (8) My backbone was
shaken violently; my feet did not stand on their pins.
(12) A voice stole in at me, calling from the throne
room. It came over to me, took hold of my right hand
(16) and picked me up. It blew a breath of life into my
face and (20) brought an increase in [my] power and
glory."

[Now] many other things like these are [in] (58.1)
his writings, including also what the angels revealed to
him and said to write (4) down for a memoir.

Again Enoch spoke in this way in (8) his Apocalypse:
"I am Enoch, the just. Great is my distress and there is
an outpouring of tears from (12) my eyes, because I have
heard the reproach which came from the mouth of the (16)
impious." Now he was saying: "With tears in my eyes and
a prayer on my (20) lips, I beheld standing before me
[seven] angels [coming down from] heaven.

---

[12]"May" refers to the month of Pharmouthi.

46

ἰδὼν δέ] αὐ|(59.1)τοὺς ἐκινήθην ὑπὸ δέ|ους ὥστε τὰ
γόνατά μου | ἀλλήλοις προσαράσσειν." | (4) καὶ πάλιν
εἶπεν οὕτως· | "ἔφη μοι εἷς τῶν ἀγγέλων | Μιχαηλ τοὔνομα·
'τού|του χάριν πρὸς σὲ ἀπεστά|(8)λην, ἵνα ὑποδείξωμέν |
σοι πάντα τὰ ἔργα καὶ ἀ|ποκαλύψωμέν σοι τὸν | τῶν εὐσεβῶν
χῶρον καὶ | (12) χῶρόν σοι δείξω τὸν τῶ[ν] | δυσσεβῶν,
καὶ ὁποῖος τυγ|χάνει ὁ τῆς τιμωρίας | τῶν ἀνόμων τόπος.'" |
(16) φησὶ δὲ πάλιν ὅτι "ἐκεῖνο[ι] | ἐπεκάθισάν με ἐπὶ
ἅ[ρ]|ματος ἀνέμου καὶ ε[ἰς] | τὰ πέρατα τῶν οὐρ[ανῶν] | (20)
ἀνήνεγκαν. καὶ το[ὺς κό]|σμους διεπεράσαμ[εν], | τόν τε
κόσμον [τοῦ θανά]|του [καὶ κόσ]μο[ν τοῦ σκό]|(60.1)τους
καὶ τοῦ πυρὸς τὸν | κόσμον. καὶ μετὰ ταῦ|τα εἰσῆξάν με
εἰς κόσμον | (4) πλουσιώτατον ὃς εὔκλε|έστατος μὲν τῶι
φωτὶ | ἐτύγχανεν, περικαλλέ|στερος δὲ ὢν εἶδον
φωσ|(8)τήρων." πάντα δὲ ἐθεώ|ρησεν καὶ ἐξήτασεν τοὺς |
ἀγγέλους, καὶ εἴ τι αὐτῶι | εἶπον, ἐνεχάραξεν αὐτοῦ |
(12) ταῖς γραφαῖς. |

ὃν τρόπον καὶ ὁ ἀπόστο|λος Παῦλος ἴσμεν ὅτι ἡρ|πάγη
ἕως τοῦ τρίτου οὐ|(16)ρ[α]νοῦ, καθὼς λέγει ἐν | [τ]ῆι πρὸς
Γαλάτας ἐπιστο|[λῆι].¹³ "Παῦλος ἀπόστολος-- | [οὐ]κ ἀπ᾿
ἀνθρώπων οὐδὲ | (20) [δι᾿ ἀν]θρώπου, ἀλλὰ διὰ | [᾿Ιησοῦ
Χ]ριστοῦ καὶ θεοῦ πατρὸς τοῦ ἐ|[γείραντ]ος αὐτὸν ἐκ τῶν |
[νεκρῶ]ν." [καὶ ἐ]ν τῆι | (61.1) πρὸς Κορινθίους δευτέ|ραι¹⁴
λέγει· "ἐλεύσομαι πά|λιν εἰς ὀπτασίας καὶ ἀπο|(4)καλύψεις
κυρίου. οἶδα ἄνθρωπον | ἐν Χριστῶι--εἴτε ἐν σώματι |

[When I saw] (59.1) them, I was shaken by fear, so that my knees knocked against each other." (4) And again he said thus: "One of the angels, Michael by name, said to me: 'For this reason I have been sent to you, (8) so that we may point out to you all the works and reveal to you the realm of the pious, and (12) that I may show you the realm of the impious and what the place of punishment of the lawless is like.'" (16) Again he said: "They set me on a chariot of wind and carried me off to the ends of the heavens. (20) [We] passed through the worlds, the world [of death] and the world of [darkness] (60.1) and the world of fire. After these things they brought me into an extremely rich world, (4) which was most glorious in its light, more splendid than the luminaries which I saw." (8) He beheld everything and carefully questioned the angels; and whatever they said to him, he would inscribe in his (12) writings.

Likewise, we know that the apostle Paul was snatched up to the third (16) heaven, just as he says in his Letter to the Galatians:[13] "Paul an apostle--not from men nor (20) [through] man, but through [Jesus] Christ and Cod the Father, who [raised] him from the [dead]." [And] in the (61.1) second Letter to the Corinthians[14] he says: "I shall go on to visions and (4) revelations of the Lord. I know a man in Christ--whether in the body or

---

[13]Cf. Gal 1:1.

[14]Cf. 2 Cor 12:1-5.

εἴτε ἐκτὸς σώματος οὐ|κ οἶδα, θεὸς οἶδεν--ὅτι ἡρπά|(8)γη
ὁ τοιοῦτος εἰς τὸν πα|ράδεισον καὶ ἤκουσεν ἄρ|ρητα ῥήματα
ἃ οὐκ ἐξὸν | ἀνθρώπωι λαλῆσαι. περὶ | (12) τοιούτου
καυχήσομαι, | περὶ δὲ ἐμαυτοῦ οὐ καυ|χήσομαι." | πάλιν
ἐν τῆι πρὸς Γαλάτας | (16) ἐπιστολῆι·[15] "δείκνυμι,
ἀ|δελφοί, τὸ εὐαγγέλι[ον] | ὃ εὐαγγελισάμην ὑμ[ῖν], | ὅτι
οὐκ ἐξ ἀνθρώπ[ου] | (20) αὐτὸ παρείληφα [οὐδὲ ἐ]|διδάχθην,
ἀλλὰ [δι' ἀπο]|καλύψεως Ἰησοῦ [Χριστοῦ." οὗτος] | δ[ὲ ὢν
ἐκ]τὸς ἐ[αυτοῦ καὶ ἀρ]|(62.1)παγεὶς εἰς τὸν τρίτον
οὐ|ρανὸν καὶ εἰς τὸν παρά|δεισον καὶ ἰδὼν καὶ ἀ|(4)κούσας
καὶ αὐτὸ τοῦτο | ἐνεχάραξεν αἰνιγματω|δῶς περί τε τῆς
ἁρπα|γῆς αὐτοῦ καὶ ἀποστολῆς | (8) τοῖς συμμύσταις τῶν |
ἀποκρύφων.

καὶ τὸ | πέρας δὲ πάντες οἱ μα|καριώτατοι ἀπόστολοι |
(12) καὶ σωτῆρες καὶ εὐαγγε|λισταὶ καὶ τῆς ἀληθείας |
προφῆται--ἕκαστος αὐ|τῶν ἐθεώρησεν καθ' ὃν[16] | (16)
[ἀ]πεκαλύφθη αὐτῶι ἐλ|[πὶ]ς ἡ ζῶσα πρὸς τὸ κήρυ|[γμ]α,
καὶ ἔγραψαν καὶ κα|[τα]λελοίπασιν καὶ ἀπέ|(20)[θεν]το εἰς
ὑπόμνησιν | [τῶν ἐ]σομένων[17] υἱῶν τοῦ | [θείου π]νεύματος
καὶ γνωσομέ|[νων τῆς] φων[ῆς αὐτο]ῦ | (63.1) τὴν αἴσθησιν.

τούτωι | τῶι τρόπωι καὶ τοῦ πανευ|φημοτάτου
ἀποστόλου, | (4) δι' οὗ καὶ ἐξ οὗ ἐλήλυθεν | ἡμῖν ἡ
ἐλπὶς καὶ ἡ κληρο|νομία τῆς ζωῆς, ἀκόλου|θόν ἐστιν[18] ἡμῖν

out of the body I do not know, God knows--that (8) this
one was snatched up into Paradise and heard secret words
which are not permitted for a man to utter. About (12)
such a one I shall boast, but about myself I shall not
boast." Again in the Letter to the Galatians:[15] (16) "I
show, brothers, the gospel which I have preached to you,
that I have not received it from man, (20) [nor] was I
taught it, but [through] a revelation of Jesus [Christ."
Now while he was outside of himself, and] (62.1) snatched
up into the third heaven and into Paradise, he both saw
and (4) heard, and it is this very thing that he recorded
in riddles about his rapture and apostleship (8) for the
fellow initiates of the mysteries.

   In conclusion, all the most blessed apostles, (12)
saviors, evangelists, and prophets of the truth--each of
them beheld insofar as[16] the (16) living hope was
revealed to him for proclamation. And they wrote down,
bequeathed, and stored up (20) for remembrance for [the]
future[17] sons of the [divine] Spirit, who will understand
the sense of [his] voice.

   (63.1) Also in this way, it is fitting[18] for the
all-praiseworthy apostle (Mani), (4) through whom and
from whom has come to us the hope and inheritance of life,

---

[15]Cf. Gal 1:11-12.

[16]Translators do not read, with Henrichs-Koenen:
καθ' ὅν | (16)<τρόπον>.

[17]Translators read the suggested reconstruction of
G. M. Browne: [τῶν ἐ]σομένων.

[18]A less likely rendering would be: "it is fitting
for us to write. . ."

γράψαι | (8) καὶ σημᾶναι τοῖς μετα|γενεστέροις πᾶσι καὶ

οἰ|κείοις τῆς πίστεως καὶ γό|νοις οὖσι πνευματικοῖς |

(12) δι᾿ ὑδάτων αὐτοῦ φανο|τάτων αὐξανομένοις, | ὡς ἂν

γνωσθῆι αὐτοῖς ἥ τε | ἁρπαγὴ αὐτοῦ καὶ ἀποκά|(16)λυψις.

ἐπιστάμεθα | γάρ, ὦ ἀδελφοί, τὸ ὑ[περ]|βάλλον τῆς σοφίας

[ὅ]|σον τυγχάνει τὸ μ[έγε]|(20)θος πρὸς ἡμᾶς κα[τὰ

ταύ]|την τὴν ἄφιξ[ιν τοῦ πα]|ρακλήτου τῆ[ς ἀληθεί]|ας.

ἣν [συ]γγιν[ώσκομεν] | (64.1) μὴ ἐξ ἀνθρώπων αὐτὸν |

προσδεδέχθαι μηδ᾿ ἐξ | ἀκοῆς τῶν βίβλων, κα|(4)θὼς καὶ

αὐτὸς ὁ πατὴρ ἡ|μῶν φησιν ἐν τοῖς συγγράμ|μασιν οἷς ἀπέ-

στειλεν εἰς | Ἔδεσαν· λέγει γὰρ οὕτως· | (8) "τὴν ἀλήθειαν

καὶ τὰ ἀ|πόρρητα ἅπερ διαλέγο|μαι--καὶ ἡ χειροθεσία

ἡ οὖ|σα παρ᾿ ἐμοί--οὐκ ἐξ ἀνθρώπων | (12) αὐτὴν παρέλαβον

ἢ σαρ|κικῶν πλασμάτων, ἀλλ᾿ οὐ|δὲ ἐκ τῶν ὁμιλιῶν τῶν |

γραφῶν. ἀλλ᾿ ὁπηνίκα | (16) θεωρήσας με οἴκτιρέν | [μου]

ὁ μακαριώτατος | [π(ατ)ὴρ] ὁ καλέσας με εἰς | [τὴν] χάριν

αὐτοῦ καὶ μὴ | (20) [βουλ]ηθείς με ἀπολέσαι | [καὶ] τοὺς

λοιποὺς τοὺς | [ἐν τῶι κ]όσμωι, ὅπως ὀρέ|[ξηι τὴν]

εὐζω[ίαν] ἐκεί|(65.1)νοις το<ῖ>ς ἑτοίμοις ἔκλε|γῆναι

αὐτῶι ἐκ τῶν δο|γμάτων, καὶ τότε τῆι | (4) αὐτοῦ χάριτι

ἀπέσπα|σέ με ἀπὸ τοῦ συνεδρίου | τοῦ πλήθους τοῦ τὴν

ἀ|λήθειαν μὴ γινώσκον|(8)τος καὶ ἀπεκάλυψέ μοι | τά τε

αὐτοῦ ἀπόρρητα | καὶ πατρὸς αὐτοῦ τοῦ ἀχράν|του καὶ

παντὸς τοῦ κό|(12)σμου. ἐξέφηνε δέ μοι | καθ᾿ ὃν ὑπῆρχον

τρόπον | πρὶν καταβολῆς κόσμου, | καὶ ὃν τρόπον ἐτέθη ἡ |

to write to us (8) and to interpret to all posterity, the
householders of faith, and those who are spiritual off-
spring, (12) increasing through his most limpid waters,
so that his rapture and revelation may be known to them.
(16) For we know, brothers, with this arrival of the
Paraclete of Truth, how great (20) the magnitude of (his)
wisdom is in relationship to us. [We acknowledge] (64.1)
that he has received it neither from men, nor from the
reading of books, just (4) as our father (Mani) himself
says in the letter which he sent to Edessa. For he says
thus: (8) "The truth and the secrets which I speak
about--and the laying on of hands which is in my posses-
sion--not from men (12) have I received it nor from
fleshly creatures, not even from studies in the Scrip-
tures. But when (16) [my] most blessed [Father], who
called me into his grace, beheld me, since he did not
(20) [wish] me [and] the rest who are [in the] world to
perish, he felt compassion, so that [he] might extend
[his] well-being to those (65.1) prepared to be chosen by
him from the sects. Then, by (4) his grace, he pulled
from the council of the many who do not recognize the truth
(8) and revealed to me his secrets and those of his unde-
filed Father and of all the cosmos. (12) He disclosed to me
how I was before the foundation of the world, and how the

(16) κρηπὶς τῶν ἔργων πάν|των ἀγαθῶν τε καὶ φαύ|λων, καὶ
ποίωι τρόπωι | ἐτέχθη (?) ἅπαν τὸ τα[ύτης] | (20) τῆς
συγκρίσε[ως κατὰ] | τούτους τ[οὺς αὐτῆς ὅ]|ρους καὶ
κ[αιρούς]." |

ἔγραψε π[άλιν οὕτω καὶ] | (66.1) εἶπεν ἐν τῶι
εὐαγγελίωι | τῆς ἁγιωτάτης αὐτοῦ ἐλ|πίδος· | (4) "ἐγὼ
Μαννιχαῖος Ἰησοῦ Χριστοῦ | ἀπόστολος διὰ θελήμα|τος θεοῦ
πατρὸς τῆς ἀληθεί|ας ἐξ οὗ καὶ γέγονα· ὃς ζῆι | (8) τε
καὶ διαμένει εἰς αἰῶνας | αἰώνων πρὸ παντὸς | μὲν ὑπάρχων,
διαμέ|νων δὲ καὶ μετὰ πάν|(12)τα. πάντα δὲ τὰ γεγο|νότα
τε καὶ γενησόμε|να διὰ τοῦ αὐτοῦ σθένους | ὑφέστηκεν.
ἐξ αὐτοῦ | (16) γὰρ τούτου πέφυκα, εἰ|μὶ δὲ καὶ ἐκ τοῦ
θελήμα|τος αὐτοῦ. καὶ ἐξ αὐτοῦ | [π]ᾶν τἀληθές μοι
ἀπε|(20)[καλύφ]θη, κἀκ τῆς ἀλη|[θείας αὐτο]ῦ τυγχάνω. |
[ἣν ἀπεκάλυψ]εν εἶδον ἀ|[λήθειαν αἰώ]νων. καὶ
ἀ|(67.1)λήθειαν μὲν ἐξέφηνα | τοῖς ἐμοῖς ξυνεμπόροις, |
εἰρήνην δὲ εὐηγγελισά|(4)μην τοῖς τῆς εἰρήνης | παισίν.
ἐλπίδα δ᾿ ἐκήρυ|ξα γένει τῶι ἀθανάτωι· | ἐκλογὴν
ἐξελεξάμην | (8) καὶ ἀτραπὸν τὴν ἐπὶ τὸ | ὕψος ὑπέδειξα
τοῖς ἀνι|οῦσι κατὰ τὴν ἀλήθειαν | τήνδε. ἐλπίδα ἐκήρυξα |
(12) καὶ τήνδε τὴν ἀποκάλυ|ψιν ἀπεκάλυψα καὶ τόδε | τὸ
ἀθάνατον εὐαγγέλιον | γέγραφα ἐνθέμενος αὐ|(16)τῶι ταῦτα
τὰ τῆς ὑπερ[ο]|χῆς ὄργια καὶ μέγιστα [ἔρ]|γα ἐκφήνας ἐν
αὐτῶι, [εἴ]|δη μέγιστα καὶ σεμν[ότα]|(20)τα ἔργων τῶν
ἰσχυ[ροτά]|των τῆς ὑ[περοχῆς. καὶ] | ταῦτα ἅπ[ερ
ἀπεκάλυψεν], | ὑπέδειξα [τοῖς ζῶσιν ἐκ] | (68.1) τῆς
θεωρίας τῆς ἀληθε|στάτης ἣν ἐθεώρησα | καὶ ἐνδοξοτάτης
ἀπο|(4)καλύψεως τῆς ἀποκα|λυφθείσης μοι."

(16) groundwork of all the works, both good and evil, was laid, and how everything of [this] aggregation was engendered (20) [according to its] present boundaries and [times]."

He wrote [thus again and] (66.1) said in the Gospel of his most holy hope: (4) "I, Mani, an apostle of Jesus Christ through the will of God, the Father of Truth, from whom I also was born, who lives (8) and abides forever, existing before all and also abiding after all. (12) All things which are and will be subsist through his power. For from this very one (16) I was begotten; and I am from his will. From him all that is true was revealed to me; (20) and I am from [his] truth. [The truth of ages which he revealed] I have seen, (67.1) and (that) truth I have disclosed to my fellow travelers; peace I have announced (4) to the children of peace, hope I have proclaimed to the immortal race. The Elect I have chosen (8) and a path to the height I have shown to those who ascend according to this truth. Hope I have proclaimed (12) and this revelation I have revealed. This immortal Gospel I have written, including in it (16) these eminent mysteries, and disclosing in it the greatest works, the greatest and most august forms (20) of the most eminently powerful works. These things which [he revealed], I have shown [to those who live from] (68.1) the truest vision, which I have beheld, and the most glorious revelation (4) revealed to me."

54

ἔφη | δ᾽ αὖ πάλιν ὡς "πάντα τὰ | ἀπόρρητα ἅπερ μοι
ὁ ἐ|(8)μὸς πατὴρ δεδώρηται, ἔκ | τε τῶν δογμάτων καὶ |
τῶν ἐθνῶν, ἔτι δὲ καὶ | τοῦ κόσμου ἀποκρύψας | (12) καὶ
σκεπάσας ὑμῖν ἀπε|κάλυψα κατὰ τὴν εὐδο|κίαν τοῦ μακαριωτά-
του | μου πατρός. καὶ εἰ πάλιν | (16) εὐδοκήσοι, αὖθις
ὑμῖν | [ἀ]ποκαλύπτω· ἡ γάρ τοι | δωρεὰ ἡ παρὰ τοῦ πατρός |
μοι δεδωρημένη με|(20)[γίσ]τη τυγχάνει καὶ | [πλουσιωτ]άτη·
εἰ γὰρ | [ὅλος ὁ κό]σμος ὑπή|[κουεν αὐτ]ῆι καὶ πάντες |
(69.1) οἱ ἄνθρωποι, ἱκανὸς ἂν ἐτύγ|χανον ἐξ αὐτοῦ τού|του
τοῦ κτήματος καὶ | (4) κέρδους οὗ μοι δεδώρη|ται ὁ ἐμὸς
πατήρ, πλουτί|σαι αὐτοὺς καὶ αὐτάρκη | καταστῆσαι τὴν
σοφί|(8)αν σύμπαντι τῶι κόσμωι." |

πάλιν ἔλεγεν ὡς "ὁπηνί|κα ηὐδόκησεν ὁ ἐμὸς | πατὴρ
καὶ πεποίηται οἰ|(12)κτιρμὸν εἰς ἐμὲ καὶ κη|δεμονίαν,
ἐξαπέστει|λεν ἐκεῖθεν σύζυγόν μου | τὸν ἀσφαλέστατον,
τὸ[ν] | (16) πάντα ἀθανασίας καρπ[όν], | ὡς ἂν οὗτος
ἐξαγοράση[ι] | με καὶ λυτρώσαιτο [ἐκ] | τῆς πλάνης τῶν
τοῦ [νό]|(20)μου ἐκείν<ου>. ἀφι[κό]|μενος δὲ πρὸς [με
κεκό]|μικέ μοι ἐλπ[ίδα τὴν ἀ]|ρίστην καὶ λ[ύτρωσιν] |
(70.1) τὴν τῆς ἀθανασίας καὶ ὑ|ποθήκας ἀληθεῖς καὶ τὴν |
χειροθεσίαν τὴν ἐκ τοῦ | (4) πατρὸς τοῦ ἐμοῦ. ἐλθὼν δὲ |
ἐκεῖνος ἐξελέξατό με | προκρίνας καὶ διέστη|σεν ἐπισπα-
σάμενος ἐκ | (8) μέσου τῶν τοῦ νόμου | ἐκείνου καθ᾽ ὃν
ἀνετρά|φην." |

πλεῖσται δὲ ὑ|περβολαὶ καὶ ἄλλαι πα|(12)ραπλήσιαι
ταύταις ὑπ[ά]ρ|χουσιν ἐν ταῖς βίβλοις | τοῦ πατρὸς ἡμῶν,
αἳ δεικνύ|ουσι τήν τε ἀποκάλυψιν | (16) αὐτοῦ καὶ ἁρπα-
γὴν τῆς | αὐτοῦ ἀποστολῆς· μεγί|[στ]η γὰρ τυγχάνει ἥδε ἡ |

Again he said: "All the secrets which my (8) Father
has given to me, while I have hidden and covered (them)
from the sects and the heathen, and still more from the
world, (12) to you I have revealed according to the
pleasure of my most blessed Father. And if again (16) he
would be pleased, once more I shall reveal (them) to you.
For, indeed, the gift which was given to me from the
Father (20) is very great and [rich]. For if [the whole]
world and all people obey [it], (69.1) I would be able
from this very possession and (4) advantage, which my
Father has given to me, to enrich them and establish
Wisdom as sufficient (8) for the entire world."

Again he said: "When my Father was pleased and had
shown (12) compassion and care for me, he sent out from
there my most unfailing Twin, the (16) entire fruit of
immortality, so that he might redeem and ransom me [from]
the error of those followers of (20) <that> Law. In
coming to [me], he has provided me with [the] best hope,
[redemption] (70.1) which is based on immortality, true
instructions, and the laying on of hands from (4) my
Father. Now when that one came, he preferred and chose
me, severed and pulled me out of (8) the midst of those
followers of that Law in which I was reared."

Now very many other extraordinary things (12) like
these are in the books of our father, which demonstrate
both his revelation (16) and the rapture of his apostleship. For very great is the

[ὐ]περβολὴ τῆς ἀφίξεως | (20) [τ]αύτης τῆς διὰ τοῦ
πα|[ρακλή]του πνεύματος τῆς ἀλη|[θείας ἀφ]ικομένης
πρὸς | [ἡμᾶς].

περὶ γὰρ τούτων | (71.1) τίνος χάριν καὶ διακ[ε]|-
κίνηται ἡμῖν ἅπαξ [πε]|πεισμένοις ὑπερβάλλ[ειν]| (4) τήνδε
τὴν ἀποστολὴν | ἐν ταῖς αὐτῆς ἀποκαλύ|ψεσιν; τούτου δὲ
χά|ριν ἐδευτερώσαμεν ἀ|(8)πὸ τῶν προγόνων ἡμῶ[ν] | πατέρων
τήν τε ἀρπα|γὴν αὐτῶν καὶ ἀποκάλυ|ψιν ἑνὸς ἑκάστου
εἶνε|(12)κα τῶν λογισμῶν τῶν | ἐνδεδυμένων τὴν ἀπι|στίαν
καὶ οἰομένων | τι περὶ ταύτης τῆς ἀπο|(16)καλύψεως καὶ
ὀπτασί[ας] | τοῦ πατρὸς ἡμῶν, ἵν᾽ εἴπ[ω]|σιν ὡς ὅτι καὶ
τῷ[ν προγό]|νων ἀποστόλων [τοιαύ]|(20)τη γέγονεν ἡ
διατα[γή]. | ὁπηνίκα γὰρ ἕκα[στος αὐ]|τῶν ἡρπάζετο, [ἄπερ
ἐθεώ]|ρει καὶ ἤκουε [ταῦτα πάν|(72.1)τα ἔ]γραφεν καὶ
ὑπεδεί|[κ]νυεν καὶ αὐτὸς αὐτοῦ | [τ]ῆς ἀποκαλύψεως
μάρ|(4)τυς ἐγένετο· οἱ δὲ μα|θηταὶ αὐτοῦ ἐγίγνοντο |
σφραγὶς αὐτοῦ τῆς ἀ|ποστολῆς. |

(8) Βαραίης ὁ διδάσκαλος |

ἡμεῖς τοίνυν, ὦ ἀδελ|φοί, παῖδες τυγχάνον|τες τοῦ
πνεύματος τοῦ πατρὸς ἡ|(12)μῶν, οἳ καὶ ταῦτα ἠκού|σαμεν
καὶ ἠκροασάμε|[θ]α, καὶ ἐν αὐτοῖς γεγηθό|[τ]ες οὕτω
γνῶμεν τὴν | (16) [παρου]σίαν αὐτοῦ πνευ|[ματο]ειδῶς, ὡς
ἀπεστά|[λη] ἐξ ἐντολῆς τοῦ πατρὸς | [αὐτοῦ] καὶ ποίωι
τρό|(20)[πωι ἐγ]εννήθη κατὰ τὸ | [σῶμα κα]ὶ ὡς ἦλθεν
αὐ|(73.1)τῶι σύζυγος αὐτοῦ ὁ σε|μνότατος καὶ διέστη[σεν] |
αὐτὸν ἐκ τοῦ νόμου κα|(4)θ᾽ ὃν ἀνετράφη αὐτοῦ [τὸ] | σῶμα.
κατὰ γὰρ τὸ εἰκ[ο]|στὸν καὶ πέμπτον ἔτος | ἀπεκαλύφθη
αὐτῷ με|(8)γαλοπρεπῶς.

abundance of this coming (20) which, through the Paraclete, the Spirit of Truth, is coming to [us].

Now concerning these things, (71.1) why are they sifted thoroughly by us, who are once and for all convinced that (4) this apostleship excels in its revelations? For this reason we have repeated (8) from our forefathers their rapture and the revelation of each one, (namely,) for the sake (12) of the considerations of those who have put on unbelief and who think they know something about this revelation (16) and vision of our father (Mani), so that they might acknowledge that [such] was also the commission given to the earlier apostles. (20) For when each of them was snatched up, [all these things which he beheld] and heard (72.1) he wrote down and set forth, and he, himself, became a witness of his own revelation. (4) But his disciples became seals of his apostleship.

(8) Baraies the Teacher

We, then, brothers, being children of the Spirit of our father (Mani), (12) who also have heard and listened to these things, thus let us rejoice in them and recognize his (16) coming spiritually, how he was sent by a command of [his] Father and in what way (20) he was begotten according to the [body, and] how his most august Twin came to him (73.1) and set him apart from the Law in (4) which his body was reared. For in his twenty-fifth year he (the Twin) was revealed magnificently to him.

58

ἔτι γὰρ αὐ|τοῦ ὑπάρχοντος ἐν τῶι | δόγματι ἐκείνωι τῶν

βα|πτιστῶν παραπλήσιος | (12) ὑπῆρχεν ἀμνάδι οἰκού|σῃ

ἐν ὀθνείαι ποίμνῃ ἢ ὃν | τρόπον ὄρνεον συνδιατρῖ|βον

ἑτέροις ὀρνέοις οὐχ [ὁ]|(16)μοφώνοις· πάντοτε γ[ὰρ] |

σὺν σοφίαι καὶ εὐμηχ[ανίαι] | ἀνεστρέφετο ἐν μέ[σωι] |

αὐτῶν πάντα ἐκεῖ[νον] | (20) τὸν χρόνον μηδ[ενὸς] | αὐτῶν

γινώσκ[οντος] | αὐτὸν τίς τυ[γχάνει] | (74.1) ἢ τί

προσεδέξατο καὶ τί αὐ|τῶι ἀπεκαλύφθη· ἀλλ' οὕ|τως αὐτὸν

εἶχον παρ' ἑαυτοῖς | (4) κατὰ τὴν τιμὴν τοῦ | σώματος. |

Ἀβιησοῦς ὁ διδάσκαλος καὶ |
Ἰνναῖος ὁ ἀδελφὸς Ζαβέδ. |

(8) ἔφη ὁ κύριος· "ὁπηνίκα μεταξὺ | αὐτῶν ὤικουν, ἐν

μιᾶι | τῶν ἡμερῶν κατέσχε | με τῆς χειρὸς Σιταῖος ὁ |

(12) πρεσβύτερος τοῦ συνε|δρίου αὐτῶν ὁ τοῦ Γαρᾶ | υἱὸς

διὰ τὸ στέργειν με | [π]άνυ καὶ ὡς υἱὸν φιλού|(16)[με]νον

ἔχειν. κατέσχεν | [με] τοίνυν τῆς χειρός-- | [οὐ]δενὸς

ἑτέρου συνόν|[τος ἡ]μῖν--καὶ πορευθεὶς | (20) [ἀνώρ]υξεν

καὶ ὑπέδει|(75.1)ξέν μοι θησαυροὺς μεγί|στους οὓς κρύφα

ἀποκει|μένους εἶχεν. ἔφη δὲ | (4) πρὸς ἐμέ· 'ἐμοὶ τυγχά-

νου|σιν οὗτοι οἱ θησαυροὶ κά|γὼ αὐτῶν τὴν ἐξουσίαν | ἔχω.

ἀπὸ δὲ τοῦ νῦν σοῦ | (8) ἔσονται· οὐδένα γὰρ ἕ|τερον

στέργω κατὰ σὲ ὧι | τούτους τοὺς θησαυροὺς | δώσω.' οὕτω

δὲ αὐτοῦ | (12) φθεγξαμένου πρὸς ἐ|μὲ ἐγὼ κατὰ τὴν

φρόνη|σιν εἶπον· 'προέλαβέ με | ὁ μακαριώτατός μου πατὴρ |

(16) καὶ δεδώρηταί μοι ἀθά|νατον θησαυρὸν μὴ π[α]|ρερχό-

μενον· ὃν ἄν τ[ις] | κληρονομήσοι, ἀθά[νατον] | (20) ζωὴν

πρὸς τοῦτο[υ[19] κομι]|εῖται.'

(8) For, while he was still in that sect of the Baptists, (12) he was like a lamb dwelling in a strange flock, or like a bird living with other birds of a (16) different song. [For] always with wisdom and skill he dwelt in their midst during all that (20) time; none of them recognized him (as to) who he [was], (74.1) or what he had received, or what had been revealed to him. Rather, they regarded him among themselves in this manner, (4) according to the estimate of the body.

Abiesous the Teacher and Innaios the Brother of Zabed

(8) The lord (Mani) said: "When I was dwelling in their midst, one day Sitaios, the (12) elder of their council, the son of Gara, took me by the hand, because he greatly loved me and regarded (me) as a beloved son. (16) He took [me], then, by the hand--no one else was with us-- and went, (20) [dug up] and showed (75.1) me very great treasures, which he kept secretly buried. He said (4) to me: 'These treasures are mine and I have control of them. From now on they will be yours. (8) For I love no one else like you, (and) to you I shall give these treasures.' When he had thus (12) spoken to me I said in my heart: 'My most blessed Father preferred me (16) and has given to me an immortal treasure which does not pass away. Whoever inherits it will receive immortal (20) life from it.'[19]

---

[19]Translators understand πρὸς τοῦτο[υ with reference to the treasure (cf. 76.19), although it could be understood with reference to the Father (translated "from him").

60

ἐγ[ὼ τοί]|νυν ἔφην Σιτα[ίωι τῶι²⁰ πρε]|σβυτέρωι· 'οἱ

πρ[ογενέστε]|(76.1)ροι οἱ κτησάμενοι τούσ|δε τοὺς γεηροὺς

θησαυ|ροὺς πρὸ ἡμῶν ποῦ τυγ|(4)χάνουσιν οἱ κληρονομή|σαντες

αὐτούς;²¹ ἰδοὺ γὰρ | ἀπέθανον καὶ ἀπώλοντο | καὶ οὐκ ἰδίους

αὐτοὺς ἔ|(8)σχον, ἀλλ᾽ οὐδὲ συναπη|νέγκαντο μεθ᾽ ἑαυτῶν.'" |

ἔφη²² δὲ πρὸς αὐτόν· "'εἰς τί | μοι τοίνυν τούτους |

(12) τοὺς θησαυροὺς τοὺς σφάλ|ματα καὶ πλημμελήμα|τα

προξενοῦντας παν|τὶ τῶι κτησαμένῳ αὐτούς; | (16) ὁ γὰρ

τοῦ θεοῦ θησαυρὸς μέ|γιστος τυγχάνει καὶ πλου|[σι]ώτατος

καὶ τῇ ζωῇ πα|ρ[ασ]τήσει πάντα τὸν αὐτὸν | (20) [κληρ]ονο-

μοῦντα.' ἰδὼν | [δὲ Σι]ταῖος μὴ πεισθεῖσαν | [ἐμοῦ] τ[ὴ]ν

φρόνησιν πρὸς | [τὴν κτῆσ]ιν ὧν ὑπεδεί|(77.1)ξατό μοι

θησαυρῶν πά|νυ ἐθαύμασεν ἐπ᾽ ἐμέ." |

Τιμόθεος |

(4) Τότε μετὰ βραχὺν καιρὸν | ἐβουλευσάμην οὕτως |

τῶι τε Σιτᾶι κἀκείνοις | τοῖς ἐκ τοῦ συνεδρίου | (8) αὐτοῦ

ἐξ ὧν ἀπεκάλυ|ψέν μοι ὁ μακαριώτατός | μου πατὴρ ἐξειπεῖν

αὐτοῖς | καὶ ὑποδεῖξαι τὴν τῆς ὁ|(12)σιότητος ἀτραπόν. |

ἐμοῦ δὲ ταῦτα διαλογιζο|μένου ὤφθη μοι ὅλος ὁ | κόσμος

γεγενημέν[ος] | (16) ὡσεὶ θάλασσα μεμ[εστω]|μένη ὑδάτων

με[λανω]|τάτων· κατα[φ]ε[ρομέ]|νας δὲ κατ᾽ αὐτ[ῆς

χιλι]|(20)άδας καὶ μυρι[άδας εἶδον] | καταποντιζ[ομένας

καὶ] | (78.1) ἀναδυνούσας

Then I spoke to Sitaios [the]²⁰ elder: 'Where are the [forefathers] (76.1) who acquired these earthly treasures before us, (4) they who inherited them?[21] For, consider, they are dead and gone and they did not keep them as their own, (8) neither did they carry (them) off with themselves.'"

He (Mani)[22] spoke to him: "'What good, then, are these (12) treasures to me, which introduce sins and offenses to everyone who acquires them? (16) For the treasure of God is very great and exceedingly rich and will bring everyone who inherits it to life.' (20) When Sitaios saw that [my] mind was not persuaded to [the acquisition] of the treasures which he showed me, (77.1) he was altogether astonished at me."

Timothy

(4) Then after a little while I (Mani) determined thus to declare to Sita and those of his council (8) what my most blessed Father had revealed to me, and to show them the path of (12) holiness. But, while I was considering these things, there appeared to me the entire world which had become (16) like a sea full of very black waters; and [I saw] thousands (20) and tens of thousands brought down into it, plunged down, (78.1) bobbing up,

---

[20]Translators read, with the critical apparatus: Σιτα[ίωι τῶι.

[21]Double apposition, probably rendering a Syriac parallelism: Cf. *ZPE* 32 (1978) 127 n. 156.

[22]Doublet of 75.23-76.9.

καὶ ἐνστρε|φομένας περὶ τὰ τέσσερα | κλίματα τῆς θαλάσσης. |

(4) εἶδον δὲ κατὰ τὸ μέσον αὐ|τῆς κρηπῖδα βεβλημέ|νην καὶ
πάνυ ὑψηλοτά|την καὶ ἐπ᾽ αὐτῆς μόνης | (8) φῶς ἀνατέλλον
καὶ ὁδὸν | ἐπ᾽ αὐτῆς κατεστρωμέ|νην καὶ ἐμαυτὸν ἐν ταύ|τηι
περιπατοῦντα. ὑπο|(12)στραφεὶς δὲ εἰς τοὐπίσω | ἐθεώρησα
Σιτᾶν κατέχον|τα ἄνδρα τινὰ ἐχόμενον | ὑπό τινος καὶ κατὰ
μέ|(16)σον τῆς θαλάσσης καὶ τοῦ | σκότους καταστρέφον|[τα]
καὶ πεσόντα καὶ ὑπο|[βρύ]χιον γενόμενον. μό|(20)[νον] δὲ
βραχύ τι τῶν τρι|[χῶν αὐ]τοῦ ἐθεώρουν ὥς|[τε λυπε]ῖσθαί
με πάνυ δι|[ὰ τὸν Σιτᾶν]. ἐκεῖνος δὲ ὁ | (79.1) ἐκρίψας
αὐτὸν ἔφη πρὸς | ἐμέ· "τίνος χάριν περὶ τοῦ | Σιτᾶ λυπῆι;
οὐ γάρ ἐστιν ἐκ | (4) τῆς σῆς ἐκλογῆς οὐδὲ ἐ|πὶ τῆς σῆς
ὁδοῦ πορεύσε|ται." ταῦτα τοίνυν ἰ|δὼν οὐδὲν αὐτῶι
ἀπεκά|(8)λυψα. ἐθεώρουν δ᾽ αὖ | πάλιν αὐτὸν ὁπηνίκα | τὸν
τῆς ἀληθείας λόγον | ὡμίλουν ἀντιπάσχον|(12)τά μου τῶι
λόγωι. |

Βαραίης ὁ διδάσκαλος |

῎Εφη ὁ κύριός μου· "ἱκανός μοι | διάλογος γεγένηται
[ἐ]|(16)ν ἐκείνωι τῶι νόμωι²³ [πρὸς] | ἕνα ἕκαστον,
ἀναΐ[σσον]|τός μου καὶ ἀνα[κρί]|νοντος αὐτοὺς [περὶ τῆς] |
(20) ὁδοῦ τοῦ θεοῦ κ[αὶ περὶ τῶν] | τοῦ σωτῆρος ἐντολ[ῶν
καὶ πε]|(80.1)ρὶ τοῦ βαπτίσματος καὶ | περὶ ὧν βαπτίζουσιν
λα|χάνων καὶ περὶ παντὸς | (4) θεσμοῦ καὶ τάξεως αὐτῶν |
καθ᾽ ἣν πορεύονται. |

"ὁπηνίκα δὲ κατέλυον καὶ | κατή<ργ>ουν αὐτῶν τοὺς |
(8) λόγους καὶ τὰ μυστήρια, | ὑποδεικνύων αὐτοῖς | ὡς
ταῦτα ἃ μετέρχονται | οὐκ ἐκ τῶν τοῦ σωτῆρος ἐντο|(12)λῶν

and spinning about the four corners of the sea. (4) I
saw in the midst of it a foundation laid and of very
great height, and over it alone (8) a light rising, and a
road laid upon it, and myself walking on this. (12) When
I turned round I beheld Sita, holding on to some man who
was held by someone else, and perishing in the (16) midst
of the sea and the darkness, after he had fallen and gone
under the surface. (20) I could see only a little bit of
his hair, so that I [was distressed] greatly on account
of [Sita]. But that one who (79.1) cast him out said to
me: "Why are you distressed about Sita? For he is not
of (4) your Elect, nor will he walk on your way." Then,
when I saw these things, I revealed nothing to him (Sita).
(8) But later, when I was preaching the Word of Truth, I
saw him opposing (12) my teaching.

Baraies the Teacher

My lord (Mani) said: "I have had enough debating
[with] each one in (16) that Law,[23] rising up and
questioning them [concerning the] (20) way of God, [the]
commandments of the Savior, (80.1) the washing, the
vegetables they wash, and their every (4) ordinance and
order according to which they walk.

"Now when I destroyed and <put to nought> their (8)
words and their mysteries, demonstrating to them that
they had not received these things which they pursue from
the commandments of the Savior,

---

[23]On νόμος as *Religionsgemeinschaft*: Cf. Henrichs,
"Mani and the Babylonian Baptists," 47-48.

64

ἐδέξαντο, τινὲς | μὲν ἐξ αὐτῶν ἐθαύμα|ζόν με, ἄλλοι δὲ
ὠργίζον|το καὶ θυμούμενοι ἔλε|(16)γον· 'μήτι εἰς τοὺς
"Ελλη|[ν]ας βούλεται πορευθῆ|[ν]αι;' ἐγὼ δ' ὁπηνίκα
ἐ|[βλ]επον αὐτῶν τὰ φρο|(20)[νήμ]ατα, ἔφασκον πρὸς |
[αὐτοὺ]ς σὺν χρηστότη|[τι· 'τοῦτο] τὸ βάπτισμα | [οὐδὲν
τ]υγχάνει ἐν ᾧ βα|(81.1)πτίζετε ὑμῶν τὰ ἐδέσμα|τα· τὸ
γὰρ σῶμα τοῦτο μι|αρόν ἐστιν καὶ ἐκ πλάσε|(4)ως μιαρότητος
ἐπλάσθη. | ὁρᾶτε δὲ ὡς ἐπάν τις καθα|ρίσῃ ἑαυτοῦ τὴν
ἐδωδὴν | καὶ ταύτης μεταλάβῃ ἤ|(8)δη βεβαπτισμένης,
φαί|νεται ἡμῖν ὅτι καὶ ἐξ αὐ|τῆς γίνεται αἷμα καὶ | χολὴ
καὶ πνεύματα καὶ σκύ|(12)βαλα τῆς αἰσχύνης καὶ | τοῦ
σώματος μιαρότης. | εἰ δέ τις κατάσχοι τὸ στό|μα ἑαυτοῦ
ἡμέρας ὀλίγ[ας]|(16)ἐκ ταύτης τῆς τροφ[ῆς], | αὐτόθι
γινώσκετα[ι ταῦ]|τα πάντα τὰ ἀπεκδ[ύμα]|τα τῆς αἰσχύνης
κ[αὶ βδε]|(20)λυρότητος ἐλλε[ίποντα] | καὶ ὑστεροῦντ[α
ἐν τῶι] | σώματι. ἐὰ[ν δ' αὖ τις] | μεταλάβῃ ἐ[δωδῆς,
τῶι] | (82.1) αὐτῶι τρόπωι πάλιν πλε|ονάζουσιν ἐν τῶι
σώμα|τι ὡς καὶ πρόδηλον εἶ|(4)ναι ὡς ἐξ αὐτῆς τῆς τρο|φῆς
πλημμυροῦσιν. | εἰ δέ τις μεταλάβοι βρώ|ματος βεβαπτισ-
μένου | (8) καὶ κεκαθαρμένου καὶ | ἐκείνου μεταλάβοι τοῦ |
ἀβαπτίστου, δῆλόν ἐστιν | ὡς τὸ κάλλος καὶ ἡ δύνα|(12)μις
τοῦ σώματος ἡ αὐ|τὴ γνωρίζεται. ὁμοί|ως δὲ καὶ ἡ βδελυρό-
της | καὶ ἡ τρὺξ τῶν ἀμφο|(16)τέρων θεωρεῖται μη|[δὲ]ν
παραλλάττουσα ἑκα|[τέ]ρας, ὥστε μὴ ἔκδηλον | [εἶν]αι
ἐκείνην τὴν βε|(20)[βαπ]τισμένην, ἣν ἀπέ|[ρριψε κ]αὶ
ἐξεδύσατο, τῆς | [ἑτέρας ἐ]κείνης τῆς ἀβα|[πτίστου].'

(12) some of them were amazed at me, but others got cross and angrily said: (16) 'Does he not want to go to the Greeks?' But, when I saw their intent, (20) I said to [them] gently: '[This] washing by which (81.1) you wash your food is of [no avail]. For this body is defiled and molded from a mold (4) of defilement. You can see how, whenever someone cleanses his food and partakes of that (food) which (8) has just been washed, it seems to us that from it still come blood and bile and flatulence and (12) excrements of shame and (the) defilement of the body. But if someone were to keep his mouth away from this (washed) food for a few days, (16) immediately all [these] offals of shame [and] loathsomeness will be known to be (20) lacking and wanting [in the] body. But if [that one] were to partake [again] of [food, in the] (82.1) same way they (i.e., the offals) would again abound in the body, so that it is manifest (4) that they swell from the food itself. But if someone else were (first) to partake of food (which is) washed (8) and cleansed, and (then) partake of that (food) which is unwashed, it is clear that the beauty and the power (12) of the body is recognized as the same (in either case). Likewise, the loathsomeness and dregs of both (types of food) (16) are seen as not differing from each other, so that what (20) has been washed, which [it (the body) rejected] and sloughed off, is not at all distinguishable from that [other] which is unwashed.'

"'καὶ τοῦτο δὲ ὃ | (83.1) καθ᾿ ἑκάστην ἡμέραν

βα|πτίζεσθε ἐν ὕδασιν οὐ|δὲν τυγχάνει· ἅπαξ γὰρ | (4)

βαπτισθέντες καὶ ἀπο|καθαρθέντες εἵνεκε[ν] | τίνος πάλιν

καθ᾿ ἑκάστη[ν] | ἡμέραν βαπτίζεσθε; | (8) ὡς καὶ ἐν τούτῳ

πρόδη|λον εἶναι σικχαίνεσθαι | ὑμᾶς καθ᾿ ἑκάστην ἡμέ|ραν

καὶ διὰ τὴν βδελυ|(12)ρότητα βαπτίζεσθαι | πρὸ τοῦ

ἀποκαθαρθῆν[αι]· | καὶ ἐν τούτῳ δὲ φαν[ε]|ρὸν εἶναι

προδηλότ[α]|(16)τα πᾶσαν τὴν μυσ[αρό]|τητα ἐκ τοῦ σώμα[τος

εἶ]|ναι. καὶ ἰδοὺ καὶ ὑ[μεῖς] | αὐτὸ ἐνεδύσασθ[ε]. |

(20) "'τοὐντεῦθεν <δ>ὲ [τί ἐστιν | ὑμῶν ἡ καθα[ρότης,

ἐξ] | ἑαυτῶν κατ[ασκέψα]|σθε. ἀδύν[ατον γάρ] | (84.1) τὰ

σώματα ὑμῶν παν|τελῶς καθαρίσαι· καθ᾿ ἑ|κάστην γὰρ ἡμέραν |

(4) κινεῖται καὶ ἵσταται τὸ | σῶμα διὰ τὰς ἐκκρίσεις | τῆς

ὑποστάθμης τὰς | [ἐ]ξ αὐτοῦ, ὡς καὶ γενέσθαι | (8) τὸ

πρᾶγμα δίχα ἐντολῆς | τῆς τοῦ σωτῆρος. ἡ τοίνυν | καθαρό-

της περὶ ἧς ἐλέ|χθη αὕτη τυγχάνει ἡ διὰ | (12) τῆς

γνώσεως, χωρισμὸς | φωτὸς ἀπὸ σκότους καὶ | τοῦ θανάτου

τῆς ζωῆς | [κα]ὶ τῶν ζώντων ὑδά|(16)[τω]ν ἐκ τῶν

τεθαμβω|[μέ]νων, καὶ ἵνα γνοῖ|[τε ὃ]τι ἑκάτερον τυγχά|[νει

...]ον ἀλλήλων καὶ κα|(20)[τ.....] τὰς τοῦ σωτῆρος

ἐντο|[λὰς ὅπω]ς ἀπολυτρώση|[..... .].[24] τὴν ψυχὴν ἐκ |

[τοῦ ὀλέθρ]ου καὶ τῆς

"'Now the fact that (83.1) you wash in water each day is of no avail. For (4) having been washed and purified once and for all, why do you wash again each day? (8) So that also by this it is manifest that you are disgusted with yourselves each day and that you must wash yourselves on account of loathsomeness (12) before you can become purified. And by this too it is clear most evidently that (16) all the foulness is from the body. And, indeed, [you] also have put it (i.e., the body) on.

(20) "'Therefore, [make an inspection of] yourselves as to [what] your purity [really is. For it is] impossible (84.1) to purify your bodies entirely--for each day the body (4) is disturbed and comes to rest through the excretions of feces from it--so that (8) the action comes about without a commandment from the Savior. The purity, then, which was spoken about, is that which comes through (12) knowledge, a separation of light from darkness, of death from life, of living waters (16) from turbid, so that [you] may know [that] each is [. . .] one another and (20) [. . .] the commandments of the Savior, [so that . . .]²⁴ might redeem the soul from [annihilation] and

---

²⁴Cf. the various possible reconstructions given in
ZPE 32 (1978) 147 n. 209:
84.19: ἀνισ]ον would be translated: "[different from]";
84.20: κα[τέχοιτε would be translated: "[may keep]";
        κα[τέχετε would be translated: "[keep]";
        κα[τ᾽ αὐτὰς] would be translated: "[according to]
        the [same] commandments";
84.21: ἀπολυτρώσῃ [ἢ γνῶσι]ς would be translated:
        "[knowledge] might redeem";
        ἀπολυτρώσῃ[ται ὑμῶ]ν would be translated: "[he]
        might redeem [your] soul."

68

ά|(85.1)πωλείας. αὕτη ἐστὶν | ἡ κατ᾽ ἀλήθειαν εὐθυτά|τη
καθαρότης ἣν παρε|(4)νεγυήθητε πρᾶξαι. ἀπε|λοήθητε δὲ
μεταβληθέ[ν]|τες ἐξ αὐτῆς καὶ κατέ|σχατε τὴν τοῦ σώματος |
(8) κάθαρσιν τοῦ μιαρωτά|του καὶ διὰ μυσαρότη|τος πεπλασ-
μένου, καὶ | δι᾽ αὐτῆς ἐτυρώθη καὶ | (12) οἰκοδομηθὲν
ἔστη.' |

"ταῦτα δέ μου εἰπόντο[ς] | πρὸς αὐτοὺς καὶ κατα[λύ]|-
σαντος καὶ καταργή[σαν]|(16)τός μου ἐκεῖνο ὅπε[ρ ἔσπευ]|δον,
τινὲς μὲν ἐξ [αὐτῶν] | εὐφήμησάν μ[ε θαυμά]|ζοντες ἐπ᾽
ἐμο[ὶ καὶ ὡσεὶ] | (20) ἀρχηγὸν καὶ δι[δάσκα]|λον ἔσχον με,
[πολὺς] | δὲ ψιθυρισμ[ὸς ἐγένετο] | ἐν ἐκείνῳ τ[ῷ
δόγμα]|(86.1)τι ἐμοῦ χάριν. τινὲς | δὲ ἐξ αὐτῶν εἶχόν με |
ὡσεὶ προφήτην καὶ δι|(4)δάσκαλον. καὶ τινες μὲν | ἐξ αὐτῶν
ἔλεγον· 'ζῶν | λόγος ᾄδεται ἐν αὐτῶι· | ποιήσωμεν αὐτὸν
διδά|(8)σκαλον τοῦ δόγματος | ἡμῶν.' ἄλλοι δὲ ἔλεγον· |
'μήτι ἄρα φωνὴ αὐτῶι | ἐλάλησεν κατὰ τὸ λελη|(12)θὸς
κἀκεῖνα ἅπερ ἀπε|κάλυψεν αὐτῶι λέγει;' | καὶ οἱ μὲν
ἔλεγον· 'μὴ κα|[τ]᾽ ὄναρ ὤφθη τι αὐτῶι, | (16) [κά]κεῖνο
ὅπερ εἶδεν λέ|[γει];' ἄλλοι δὲ ἔλεγον· 'μή|[τι οὖτ]ός
ἐστιν περὶ οὗ | [ἐπροφ]ήτευσαν οἱ διδά|(20)[σκαλο]ι
ἡμῶν λέγοντες· | "[ἀναστή]σεταί τις ἤ[θε|[ος ἐκ μέσ]ου
ἡμῶν καὶ | [διδάσκα]λος νέος π[ρο]σε|(87.1)λεύσεται ὡς
καὶ κινῆσαι | ἡμῶν τὸ πᾶν δόγμα, ὃν | τρόπον οἱ πρόγονοι
ἡμῶν | (4) πατέρες ἐφθέγξαντο | περὶ τῆς ἀναπαύσεως | τοῦ
ἐνδύματος."' ἄλλοι | δὲ ἔλεγον· 'μὴ ἄρα πλάνη | (8) ἐστὶν
ἡ ἐν αὐτῶι φθεγ|γομένη καὶ βούλεται | τὸ ἔθνος ἡμῶν
ἀποπλα|νῆσαι καὶ διχάσαι τὸ δό|(12)γμα;' ἄλλοι δὲ ἐξ
αὐτῶν | φθόνου καὶ ὀργῆς ἐπλη|ρώθησαν, ἐξ ὧν τινες |
ἐψηφίζοντο θάνατο[ν]. |

(85.1) destruction. This is in truth the genuine purity, which you (4) were commended to do; but you departed from it and began to bathe, and have held on to the purification of the body, (8) (a thing) most defiled and fashioned through foulness; through it (i.e., foulness) it (the body) was coagulated and (12) having been founded came into existence.'

"When I said these things to them, and destroyed and demolished (16) that very thing they [were zealous for], some of [them], marveling at me, praised me and regarded me [as] (20) a leader and teacher; but [there arose much] slander in that [sect] (86.1) on account of me. Some of them regarded me as a prophet and (4) teacher. Some of them were saying: 'A living word is uttered by him; let us make him a teacher (8) of our doctrine.' Others were saying: 'Has a voice really spoken to him in secret (12) and does he say those things which it revealed to him?' Some were saying: 'Did something appear to him in a dream (16) [and] does he say that which he saw?' Others were saying: 'Is this really the one about whom our teachers [prophesied], (20) saying, "A certain young man will [rise up from] our [midst] and a new [teacher] will come forth (87.1) to overturn all our teaching in the way our forefathers (4) spoke concerning the Rest of the Garment."' Others were saying: 'Surely, then, is it not error (8) that speaks through him, and does he not wish to lead our people astray and divide our teaching?' (12) Others of them were filled with jealousy and rage, some of whom were voting for (my) death.

(16) ἄλλοι δὲ ἔλεγον· 'ο̣ὖτ̣ό̣[ς ἐ]|στιν ὁ ἐχϑρὸς το[ῦ
νόμου] | ἡμῶν.' καὶ οἱ μὲ[ν ἔλεγον]· | 'εἰς τὰ ἔϑνη
βούλ[εται πο]|(20)ρευϑῆναι καὶ Ἑλ̣[ληνικὸν] | ἄρτον
φαγεῖν· [ἠκού]|σαμεν γὰρ αὐ[τοῦ λέγον]|τος· "δέον ἐσ[τὶν
Ἑλληνι]|(88.1)κοῦ ἄρτου μεταλαμβά|νειν." ὁμοίως δὲ καὶ
πο|τοῦ καὶ σίτου καὶ τῶν | (4) λαχάνων καὶ ὀπώρας | <ὧν>
οἱ πατέρες ἡμῶν καὶ | διδάσκαλοι ἠσφαλίσαν|το μὴ ἐσϑίειν
οὖτός φη|(8)σιν ἀκόλουϑον εἶναι αὐ|τῶν μεταλαμβάνειν. |
ὁμοίως δὲ καὶ τὸ βάπτισμα | ἐν ὧι βαπτιζόμεϑα | (12)
καταλύει καὶ οὐ βαπτί|ζεται ὡς ἡμεῖς, ἀλλ' οὐ|[δ]ὲ τὸ
ἄριστον αὐτοῦ βα|[π]τίζει καϑ' ἡμᾶς.'

"τότε | (16) [τοῦ]ν̣υ̣[ν] Σιτᾶν ἰδὼν καὶ οἱ | [ἑταῖρ]οι
αὐτοῦ ὡς εἰς πει|[ρασμὸ]ν̣ αὐτῶν οὐχ ἥξω, | [ἀλλὰ] κατὰ
βραχὺ βρα|(20)[χὺ κα]ταλύω καὶ καταρ|[γῶ τὸν] σῶν αὐτῶν
νό|[μον καὶ] τὰ ἐδέσματα ἅ|[περ ἀπέκ]ριναν καὶ τὸ | (89.1)
βάπτισμα μὴ βαπτιζό|μενον ὁμοίως αὐτοῖς, | ἰδόντές με ἐν
τούτοις | (4) πᾶσιν ἀνϑεστῶτα αὐτοῖς | τότε Σιτᾶν καὶ τὸ
πλῆϑος | τῶν ἑταίρων αὐτοῦ πρε|σβυτέρων σύνοδον ἐ|(8)ποιή-
σαντο ἐμοῦ χάριν. | ἐκάλεσαν δὲ καὶ τὸν οἰκοδε|σπότην
Παττίκιον καὶ | εἶπον αὐτῷ· 'ὁ υἱός σου ἐ|(12)ξετράπη τοῦ
νόμου ἡ|μῶν καὶ εἰς τὸν κόσμον | βούλεται πορευϑῆνα[ι]· |
καὶ σίτινον ἄρτ[ο]ν κα[ὶ ὀ]|(16)πώραν καὶ λάχανα [ἃ
ἀφο]|ρίζομεν ἡμεῖς κα[ὶ οὐκ ἐ]|σϑίομεν, τούτοις [πᾶσιν] |
οὐκ ἐξακολουϑεῖ [καὶ φη]|(20)σι δέον εἶναι κιν̣[ῆσαι]²⁵ |
ταῦτα.

(16) Others were saying: '[He] is the enemy of our [Law].'
Some [were saying]: '[He] wishes to go to the Gentiles (20)
and eat [Greek] bread, for we [have heard him saying], "It
is necessary to partake of [Greek] bread." (88.1) Likewise, he says it follows to partake of drink, bread, (4)
vegetables, and fruit, <which> our fathers and teachers
enjoined (us) not to eat. (8) Likewise, the washing by
which we wash ourselves (12) he destroys and does not
wash himself like us, nor does he wash his food as we do.'

"So, (16) [then], when Sita and his [companions] saw
that I would not give in to their [testing, but] (that)
little by little (20) I was destroying and bringing to
nought their own [Law and] the food [which] they
[rejected], and (that I) (89.1) was not practicing the
washing as they (were); when they saw me opposing them in
(4) all these things, then Sita and the group of his
fellow presbyters set up a synod (8) on my account. They
also summoned the master of the house, Pattikios, and
said to him: 'Your son (12) has turned aside from our
Law and wishes to go into the world. Wheat bread and
(16) fruit and vegetables [which] we [exclude] and do
[not] eat, [all] these things he does not follow [and]
says (20) it is necessary [to overturn][25] these things.

---

[25]Translators read the suggested reconstruction of
A. Groton: κιν[ῆσαι].

72

ἀλλο[ιοῖ²⁶ τὸ βάπτι]|σμα ὃν τρόπο[ν ἡμῖν βα]|πτίζεται.
['Ελληνικὸν] | (90.1) δὲ ἄρτον βούλεται ἐσθί|ειν.'
Παττίκιος δὲ | διὰ τὸ τεθεωρηκέναι | (4) αὐτῶν τὸν
μέγιστον | θόρυβον ἔφη πρὸς αὐ|τούς· 'καλέσατε ὑμεῖς |
αὐτὸν καὶ πείσατε.'

"καὶ | (8) τότε καλέσαντές με | πρὸς αὐτοὺς
συνηθροι|σμένοι ἔφασαν πρὸς | ἐμέ· 'ἐκ νεότητος πρὸς |
(12) ἡμᾶς ὑπάρχων καλῶς | διῆγες ἔν τε ταῖς τάξε|[σ]ιν
καὶ ἀναστροφαῖς | τοῦ νόμου ἡμῶν· ὡς | (16) [νύ]μφη
κατεσταλμέ|[νη] ὑπῆρχες ἐν μέσωι | [ἡμ]ῶν. νῦν τί σοι
γέγο|[νεν] ἢ τί σοι ὤφθη; ἀν|(20)[θίστ]ασαι γὰρ ἡμῶν τῶι |
[νόμωι] καὶ καταλύεις | [καὶ κα]ταργεῖς ἡμῶν | [τὸ δόγμα.
ἤ]μειψας δὲ τὴν | (91.1) πορείαν σου τῆς ἡμε|τέρας. τὸν
μὲν γὰρ πατέρα | σου διὰ μεγίστης τι|(4)μῆς ἔχομεν. τίνος
οὖν | χάριν νῦν καταλύεις | τὸ βάπτισμα τοῦ νόμου | ἡμῶν
καὶ τῶν πατέ|(8)ρων ἐν ὧι ἀναστρεφόμε|θα ἐκ πάλαι; κατα-
λύεις | δὲ καὶ τὰς ἐντολὰς τοῦ | σωτῆρος· βούλει δὲ καὶ
ἄρτον | (12) σίτινον ἐσθίειν καὶ λά|χανα ἅπερ ἡμεῖς οὐκ
ἐ|σθίομεν. τίνος <δ>ὲ χ[ά]|ριν οὕτως ἀναστρέ[φηι] | (16)
μὴ ὑπείκων πρὸς [τὸ] | γεωργεῖν τὴν γῆ[ν ὃν] | τρόπον
ἡμεῖς;' |

"τότε ἔφην πρὸς [αὐτούς·] | (20) 'μὴ γένοιτό μο[ι
τὰς ἐν]|τολὰς τοῦ σωτῆρος [καταλύ]|ειν. εἰ δὲ δι[ὰ
σίτι]|νον ἄρτον [ὀνειδί]|(92.1)ζετέ με διὰ τὸ εἰρηκέ|ναι
με· "δέον ἐστὶν ἐσθί|ειν ἐξ αὐτοῦ,"

[He][26] makes of no avail [the washing] in the way it is practiced [by us]. (90.1) And he wishes to eat [Greek] bread.' Now Pattikios, because he had beheld (4) their very great uproar, said to them: 'Summon him yourselves and persuade (him).'

(8) "Then, when they summoned me to them, they gathered around and said to me: 'From youth you have been with (12) us, doing well in the ordinances and customs of our Law. You have been like (16) a demure [young girl] in our midst. Now what has happened to you, what has appeared to you? (20) For you [oppose] our [Law] and destroy [and] bring to nought our [teaching]. You have changed (91.1) your lifestyle from ours. We hold your father in greatest (4) esteem. Why, then, do you now destroy the washing of our Law and that of the fathers, (8) in which we have walked from of old? You even destroy the commandments of the Savior; you even wish to eat wheat bread (12) and vegetables which we do not eat. Why do [you] live so, (16) not submitting to till the earth like us?'

"Then I said to [them]: (20) 'In no way would I [destroy the] commandments of the Savior. But, if you [reproach] me [on account of wheat] bread, (92.1) because I have said, "It is necessary to eat of it,"

---

[26]W. Burkert suggests a different reconstruction: ἀλλ᾽ ο[ὐδὲ τὸ βάπτι]σμα ὃν τρόπο[ν ἡμεῖς βα]πτίζεσθαι, which would be translated: "but he does [not] wash himself in the way [we] do."

τοῦτο ὁ σωτὴρ | (4) πεποίηκεν, ὡς καὶ γέ|γραπται ὡς
ὀπηνίκα εὐ|λογήσας παρέσχετο τοῖς | αὐτοῦ μαθηταῖς, "ἐπὶ
ἄρ| (8)τον εὐλόγησεν καὶ δέ|δωκεν αὐτοῖς." ἐκεῖ|νος τοίνυν
ὁ ἄρτος οὐ|κ ἦν ἐκ σίτου; δείκνυ|(12)σι δὲ ὡς μετὰ
τελωνῶν | καὶ εἰδωλολατρῶν ἀ|νεκλίθη. ὁμοίως δὲ καὶ |
[ἐ]ν τῆι οἰκίαι Μάρθας καὶ | (16) [Μα]ρίας ἐκλίθη.
ὀπηνί|[κα] εἶπεν αὐτῶι ἡ Μάρ|[θα· "κύρι]ε, οὐ μέλει σοι
περὶ | [ἐμο]ῦ ἵνα εἴπης τῆι ἀ|(20)[δελφ]ῆι μου ἀντι-
λαβέ|[σθαι μο]υ;" ὁ σωτὴρ ἔφη | [πρὸς αὐτ]ήν· "Μαρία τὴν |
[ἀγαθὴν με]ρίδα ἐπελέ|(93.1)ξατο καὶ οὐκ ἀφαιρε|θήσεται
ἀπ' αὐτῆς."²⁶ᵃ | σκοπεῖτε τοίνυν ὡς καὶ | (4) οἱ μαθηταὶ
τοῦ σωτῆρος ἄρτον | ἀπὸ γυναικῶν καὶ εἰδ[ω]|λολατρῶν
ἤσθιον καὶ | οὐ διεχώρισαν ἄρτον | (8) ἄρτου, ἀλλ' οὐδὲ
λάχα|νον λαχάνου, οὐδὲ ἐν | τῆι ἐργασίαι καὶ γεωργί|αι
τῆς γῆς ἐργαζόμεν[οι] | (12) ἤσθιον ὃν τρόπον τή|μερον
διαπράττεσθ[ε]. | ὁμοίως δὲ ὀπηνίκα ἀ[πέ]|στειλεν αὐτοῦ
τοὺ[ς μα]|(16)θητὰς ὁ σωτὴρ καθ' ἕκ[αστον] | τόπον κηρύξαι,
[οὔτε] | μύλον οὔτε κλί[βανον] | συνεπεφέρου[το με]|(20)τ'
αὐτῶν, ἀ[λ]λ' [..... .]|γοντο²⁷ περ[ιβολὴν] | μίαν ἐκ
το[..... ..] | λαμβάν[. . .].'" |

(94.1) Ζα...[. . .]²⁸ |

Εἰ τοίνυν περὶ τοῦ βαπτί|σματος κατηγορεῖτε | (4)
μου, ἰδοὺ πάλιν ἐκ τοῦ | νόμου ὑμῶν δείκνυ|μι ὑμῖν καὶ
ἐξ ἐκείνων τῶν | ἀποκαλυφθέντων τοῖς | (8) μείζοσιν
ὑμῶν ὅτι οὐ | δέον ἐστὶ βαπτίζεσθαι. |

this the Savior (4) has done; as it is written, that when
he had blessed (it) and shared (it) with his disciples,
"over (8) bread he said a blessing and gave (it) to them."
Was not that bread from wheat? It (Scripture) points out
(12) that he reclined to eat with tax collectors and
idolaters. Likewise, he also reclined to eat in the house
of Martha and (16) Mary on the occasion when Martha said
to him: "[Lord], do you not care (enough) for [me] so as
to tell my [sister to] (20) help [me]?", the Savior said
[to] her: "Mary has chosen the [good] portion (93.1) and it
will not be taken away from her."[26a] Consider, moreover,
how even (4) the disciples of the Savior ate bread from
women and idolaters and did not separate bread (8) from
bread, nor vegetable from vegetable; nor did they eat,
while laboring in the toil and tilling of the land, (12) as
you do today. Likewise, when the Savior sent his (16)
disciples out to preach in [each] place, [neither] mill
nor [oven] did [they] carry [with] (20) them, but [made
haste],[27] taking one [garment] from [. . .].'"

(94.1) Za[chias][28]

If, then, you accuse me (Mani) about the washing,
(4) look, again I prove to you from your Law and from
those things revealed to your (8) leaders that it is not
necessary to wash.

[26a]Cf. Luke 10:38-42.

[27]Editors suggest: [ἠπεί]γοντο.

[28]For reconstruction: Cf. *ZPE* 32 (1978) 178 n. 269.

δείκνυσι γὰρ ᾿Αλχασαῖος | ὁ ἀρχηγὸς τοῦ νόμου
ὑ|(12)μῶν· πορευομένου | γὰρ αὐτοῦ λούσασθαι εἰς | ὕδατα
εἰκὼν ἀνδρὸς ὤ|φθη αὐτῶι ἐκ τῆς πη|(16)[γ]ῆς τῶν ὑδάτων
λέγου|[σα] πρὸς αὐτόν· "οὐκ αὐ|[τάρ]κως ἔχει τὰ ζῷά σου |
[πλή]ττειν με, ἀλλὰ καὶ | (20) [αὐτὸς] σὺ καταπονεῖς |
[.....].[..]ον²⁹ καὶ τὰ ὕ|[δατά μου ἀ]σεβεῖς;" ὥσ|[τε
θαυμάσ]αι τὸν ᾿Αλχα|(24)[σαῖον καὶ ε]ἰπεῖν πρὸς | (95.1)
αὐτήν· "[ἡ] πορνεία καὶ ἡ μι|αρότης καὶ ἡ ἀκαθαρσία | τοῦ
κόσμου ἐπιρρίπτε|(4)ταί σοι καὶ οὐκ ἀπαυδᾷς, | ἐπ᾿ ἐμοὶ
δὲ λυπῇ;" ἔφη | πρὸς αὐτόν· "εἰ καὶ οὗτοι | πάντες οὐκ
ἔγνωσάν | (8) με τίς τυγχάνω, σὺ ὁ | φάσκων λάτρης εἶναι |
καὶ δίκαιος διὰ τί οὐκ ἐ|φύλαξάς μου τὴν τι|(12)μήν;"
καὶ τότε κινηθε[ὶς ὁ] | ᾿Αλχασαῖος οὐκ ἐλούσ[α]|το εἰς
τὰ ὕδατα.

καὶ π[ά]|λιν μετὰ πολὺν ἐβου[λή]|(16)θη λούσασθαι
εἰς τ[ὰ ὕδα]|τα καὶ ἐνετείλατ[ο τοῖς] | μαθηταῖς αὐτ[οῦ
ἐπιτη]|ρῆσαι τόπον ἔχ[οντα] | (20) ὕδατα μὴ συ[χνὰ ἵνα] |
λούσηται· ε[ὗρον δ᾿ οἱ] | μαθηταὶ α[ὐτοῦ τὸν τό]|(96.1)πον
αὐτῶι. μέ[λλον]|τος δὲ αὐτοῦ λού[σασθαι] | πάλιν ἐκ
δευτέρου ὤ|(4)φθη αὐτῷ εἰκὼν ἀν|δρὸς ἐκ τῆς πηγῆς ἐκεί|νης
λέγουσα αὐτῷ· "ἡμεῖς | κἀκεῖνα τὰ ὕδατα τὰ | (8) ἐν τῇ
θαλάσσῃ ἓν τυγχάνο|μεν· ἦλθες οὖν καὶ ἐν|ταῦθα ἁμαρτῆσαι
καὶ | πλῆξαι ἡμᾶς." πάνυ δὲ | (12) τρομάσας καὶ κινη|θεὶς
ὁ ᾿Αλχασαῖος τὸν πη|[λ]ὸν τὸν ἐπὶ τῆς κεφα|[λῆ]ς αὐτοῦ
εἴασεν ξηραν|(16)[θῆ]ναι καὶ οὕτως ἀπέ|[δε]ιξεν.³⁰ |

For Elchasai, the founder of your Law, points this
out: (12) when he was going to bathe in the waters, an
image of a man appeared to him from the source (16) of
the waters, saying to him: "Is it not enough that your
animals injure me, but (20) do you [yourself] also mis-
treat [me without reason]²⁹ and profane [my waters]?" So
Elchasai [marveled (24) and] said to it: (95.1) "Forni-
cation, defilement, and impurity of the world are thrown
into (4) you and you do not refuse (them), but are you
grieved with me?" It said to him: "Granting that all
these have not recognized (8) me (as to) who I am, you,
who say that you are a servant and righteous, why have
you not guarded my honor?" (12) And then Elchasai was
upset and did not bathe in the waters.

Again, a long time after, he wished (16) to bathe in
the waters. He commanded his disciples to [look out for]
a place not [having much] (20) water, [so that] he might
bathe. [His] disciples [found such a] place (96.1) for
him. As he [was about to] bathe, (4) the image of a man
appeared to him again, a second time, from that source,
saying to him: "We and those waters (8) in the lake are
one. You have come, therefore, even here to wrong and
injure us." (12) Trembling greatly and upset, Elchasai
allowed the mud upon his head to dry, (16) and thus he
pointed it out.³⁰

---

²⁹Translators read, with the critical apparatus:
[με παρ]ὰ [λόγ]ον.

³⁰W. Burkert suggests: ἀπέ[σμ]ηξεν, which would be
translated: "he wiped it off."

[πάλιν δ]είκνυσιν ὅτι εἶ|[χεν ἄρ]οτρα ὁ ᾿Αλχασαῖος |

(20) [ἀποκείμ]ενα καὶ ἐπορεύ|[θη εἰς α]ὐτά. ἐφθέγξα|[το

δ᾿ ἡ γῆ λ]έγουσα αὐτ[ῷ]· | (97.1) "[τί] πράττ[ε]τε ἐξ ἐμοῦ |

[τ]ὴν ἐργασίαν ὑμῶν;" | [ὁ δ]ὲ ᾿Αλχασαῖος δεξάμε|(4)νος

χοῦν ἐκ τῆς γῆς ἐ|κείνης τῆς λαλησάσης | πρὸς αὐτὸν κλαίων

κα|τεφίλησε καὶ ἐπέθηκε | (8) τῶι κόλπωι καὶ ἤρξα[το] |

λέγειν· "αὕτη ἐστὶν ἡ | σάρξ καὶ αἷμα τοῦ κυρίου μου." |

ἔφη δ᾿ αὖ πάλιν ὅτι εὗρεν | (12) τοὺς μαθητὰς αὐτοῦ |

᾿Αλχασαῖος πέπτοντας | ἄρτους ὡς καὶ λαλῆσαι | τὸν ἄρτον

πρὸς τὸν [᾿Αλ]|(16)χασαῖον· ὃς δὲ ἐνετε[ίλα]|το μηκέτι

πέπτει[ν]. |

πάλιν δείκνυσιν ὅ[τι Σαβ]|βαῖος ὁ βαπτιστὴ[ς τὰ] |

(20) λάχανα ἀπέφερ[ε πρὸς] | τὸν πρεσβύτε[ρον τῆς] |

[π]όλεως. [κ]αὶ ε[ὐθέως ἐ]|[κ]εῖνο τ[ὸ φορτίον

εἶ]|(98.1)[π]εν αὐτῶι· "οὐκ εἶ δίκ[αι]|ος; οὐ καθαρὸς

τυγχάν[εις]; | τίνος χάριν ἀπάγεις ἡ|(4)μᾶς πρὸς τοὺς

πόρνους;" | ὡς κινηθῆναι τὸν Σαβ|βαῖον δι᾿ ἃ ἤκουσεν καὶ |

ἀνθυποστρέψαι τὰ λά|(8)[χ]ανα.

[π]άλιν δείκνυσιν ὡς με|τὰ ᾿Αϊανοῦ τοῦ βαπτι|στοῦ

τοῦ ἀπὸ Κωχῆς | (12) φοῖνιξ συνελάλησεν | καὶ ἐνετείλατο

αὐτῶι | εἰπεῖν τῶι κυρίωι <αὐτ>οῦ· "μὴ | [δ]ὴ ἐκκόψῃς διὰ

τὸ κλέ|(16)[π]τεσθαί μου τοὺς καρ|[π]ούς, ἀλλ᾿ ἔασόν με

τὸ | [ἔτο]ς τοῦτο. καὶ τούτωι | [τῶι] ἐνιαυτῶι δώσω σοι |

(20) [καρπ]οὺς ἀναλογοῦν|[τας το]ῖς κλαπεῖσιν, ἔ|[τι δὲ

ἐ]ν π[ᾶσ]ι τοῖς ἐτέ|[ροις ἔτεσιν]." ἐνετεί|(99.1)λα[το] δὲ

κἀκείνωι τῶι | ἀνθρώπωι τῷ κλέπτον|τι τοὺς καρποὺς αὐτοῦ |

(4) εἰπεῖν· "μὴ ἔλθῃς τῷδε | τῶι καιρῶι ἀποκλέψα[ι] | μου

τοὺς καρπούς. ε[ἰ] | δὲ ἔλθοις, ἐκρίπτω σε | (8) ἐκ τοῦ

ὕψους μου καὶ ἀ|ποθανεῖσαι." |

[Again] he (Mani) demonstrates that Elchasai [had ploughs (20) in storage] and went [to] them. [The earth] spoke [to him], saying: (97.1) "[Why do you make] your living from me?" Elchasai, having taken (4) soil from that earth which spoke to him, wept, kissed (it) and placed (it) upon (8) his breast and began to say: "This is the flesh and blood of my Lord."

He (Mani) said again that Elchasai found (12) his disciples baking bread. The bread spoke with (16) Elchasai, and he commanded (them) to bake no longer.

Again he (Mani) points out [that] Sabbaios, the Baptist, (20) was carrying vegetables [to] the elder of [the] city. [And immediately] that [produce said] to (98.1) him: "Are you not righteous? Are [you] not pure? Why do you carry us away (4) to the fornicators?" Thus Sabbaios was upset on account of what he heard and returned the (8) vegetables.

Again he (Mani) points out that a date-palm tree spoke with Aianos, the Baptist from Koche, (12) and commanded him to say to <its> lord: "Don't cut (me) down because (16) my fruit is stolen, but grant me this [year]. And in [the] course of this year I shall give you (20) [fruit] proportionate to [what] has been stolen, [and in all] the [other years hereafter]." (99.1) But [it] also commanded (him) to say to that man who was stealing its fruit: (4) "Do not come at this season to steal my fruit away. If you come, I shall hurl you down (8) from my height and you will die."